SPT 27

CISTERCIAN FATHERS SERIES: NUMBER THIRTEEN

BERNARD OF CLAIRVAUX

Volume Five

TREATISES II

CISTERCIAN FATHERS SERIES: NUMBER THIRTEEN

THE WORKS OF BERNARD OF CLAIRVAUX

Volume Five

Treatises II

CISTERCIAN PUBLICATIONS
CONSORTIUM PRESS
Washington, D.C.
1974

The translations presented here are based on the critical Latin edition prepared by Jean Leclercq OSB and Henri Rochais under the sponsorship of the Order of Cistercians and published by Editiones Cistercienses, Piazza Tempio di Diana 14, I-00153 Rome, Italy.

De gradibus humilitatis et superbiae, OB III, 13-59.
Liber de diligendo deo, OB III, 119-154.

Cistercian Fathers Series   ISBN 0-87907-000-5
The Works of Bernard of Clairvaux   ISBN 0-87907-100-1
This volume   ISBN 0-87907-113-3

Library of Congress Catalog Card Number: 74-4147

Ecclesiastical permission to publish this book has been received from Bernard Flanagan, Bishop of Worcester, September 28, 1972.

CONTENTS

THE STEPS OF HUMILITY AND PRIDE

ON LOVING GOD

THE STEPS OF HUMILITY AND PRIDE

INTRODUCTION

THE STEPS OF HUMILITY is Bernard of Clairvaux's first published work.[1] And yet surely it is not the work of an amateur as both its immediate popularity and its continued popularity through the centuries clearly attest.[2] It has been published in English translation more frequently than any of his other works with the possible exception of his treatise, *On Loving God.*[3]

The title of the treatise does not really prepare the reader for what is to be found in it.[4] This is not a new discovery. Bernard's first critics said the same. And the sensitive young Abbot felt the need to defend himself in his *Retractatio.*[5]

---

1. Godfrey of Langres, to whom this Treatise is addressed, in the Fourth Book of the *Life of St Bernard (S. Bernardi Vita Prima)* speaks of "his first work concerning the steps of humility."—c. 8, PL 185:320. For a fuller treatment of this question and indeed for an excellent introduction in general, see the Introduction in *S. Bernardi Opera* (hereafter OB) ed. J. Leclercq, H. Rochais (Rome:Editiones Cistercienses) vol. 3 (1963) pp. 3-11. On this particular point see also, J. Leclercq, "Le premier traité authentique de saint Bernard?" *Recueil d'études sur saint Bernard et ses écrits* (Rome:Edizioni di Storia e Letteratura) vol. 2 (1966) pp. 51-67, reprinted from *Revue d'histoire ecclésiastique* 48 (1953): 196-210.

2. This is evident from the diffusion of the mss. See OB 3:4ff.

3. See the Bibliography below, pp. 133-135.

4. Mills echoes the sentiment of many when he says in his Introduction: "The title of the book is somewhat misleading." Saint Bernard, *The Twelve Degrees of Humility and Pride,* tr. B. R. V. Mills (London: SPCK, 1929), p. viii.

5. "Some have objected to the title: "The Steps of Humility," on the ground that I have described the steps not of humility but of pride. They must not have understood or have not noticed my note at the end where I briefly explain the title."—below, p. 25.

1

THE RETRACTATIO

A tradition going back to manuscripts contemporary with Bernard himself places the *Retractatio*[6] at the head of the treatise.[7] It is certainly an important document, not so much because of the correctives it brings to the text as for what it tells us about the author. It assures us that he "practices what he preaches." It may be spirited, but it certainly is the expression of a truly humble man. Where he had been wrong, he readily confessed it. He had no desire to conceal it; he wanted to right the wrong. We see a man who readily accepted himself as fallible, a man genuinely and courageously self-possessed. He did not have to be right. This same spirit is evinced in his willingness to set forth a personal opinion as a personal opinion. Yet his was true humility, based on truth. Where his critics are wrong he was not ready to make any false protestations but firmly stood his ground. All the virtues are interconnected; the truly humble man is also truthful and courageous.

But the *Retractatio* tells us something else about the author, something it is well to keep in mind when reading not only this treatise but all his subsequent writings. Bernard tells us here that when he quoted Scripture he depended on his memory, and not a verbal memory, but rather a general sense of the passage.[8] This was true even in a case where the text in question was the basis of his whole line of reasoning. Thus as we

---

6. The English "Retractation" does not do justice to the content of the Latin word; it is rather a reconsidering of the matter—in this case, in the light of some objections, which are answered with both a retractation and a spirited defense.

7. See OB 3:5ff.

8. "I quoted, as I thought, the text and then found that it was not in the Gospel at all. I had no intention of falsifying the text but I was depending on my memory of the general sense of the passage and made a slip in the words."—below, p. 25. Dom Jean Leclercq has pointed out to me that Wordsworth and White in their *Novum Testamentum latine* (Oxford, 1889-98) indicate that at Mk 13:32, the text Bernard quoted, *filius hominis* (Son of Man), is found in some mss, including the *Book of Armagh (Dublinensis)* and the *Book of Kells* (Dublin) (see Wordsworth and White, 1:253) so a certain "Irish" tradition may have influenced the text first quoted by Bernard. I am grateful to Dom Jean Leclercq for this indication and for the other helpful suggestions he made after reading this Introduction.

read St Bernard we should not be surprised at times to find
that his Scriptural texts are not exactly those found in our
Bibles. He may have had in mind the Vulgate or the Old Latin
version,[9] or more likely texts from these employed in the liturgy where they are sometimes adapted to the context. Or he
may, as he admits here, have been speaking from the general
sense of the passage. Bernard was not usually too concerned
with the literal sense of the Scriptural texts he employed
(though sometimes he certainly was, as we can see from this
treatise). He was quite ready to leave this husk to get at the
inner meat, the typological meaning.[10] And even there, for this
man so typically monastic, it was the practical moral sense
that most interested him—what he and his brethren could be
doing to respond to the reality revealed—rather than the allegorical or anagogic meanings.[11]

The *Retractatio* also tells us something about the diffusion
of Bernard's works. We do not know exactly when it was writ-

9. Watkin Williams in his Preface quotes Dr White, Dean of Christ Church: ". . .
his considered opinion is that St Bernard 'probably used an ordinary Vulgate text
which had preserved a certain number of Old Latin readings, as so many of the
Vulgate mss did; and also that he often quoted from memory.' " Williams goes on
to say, still depending on White: "a salient instance of the former would be the
addition of 'quanto magis' in John xiii. 15." There is no indication that White
considered the possibility that Bernard received some of his Scripture sources
through the liturgy. See *Select Treatises of St. Bernard of Clairvaux*, Cambridge
Patristic Texts, ed. W. Williams and B. Mills (Cambridge: University Press, 1926)
pp. viif.

10. "Let us now endeavor, under the guidance of the Spirit of truth, to extract
the mystical meaning which lies underneath the rind of the letter."—SC 51:2, OB 2
(1958) p. 84; CF 31; "Such is the literal sense, the portion of the Jews. But for
me, following the counsel of the Lord I will search for the treasure of spirit and
life hidden in the profound depths of these inspired utterances."—SC 73:1-2; OB
2:234; CF 40.

11. "I had indeed hoped that the discussion of the mystical sense of our text
would not have detained us so long. I actually thought that one sermon would
suffice, and that passing quickly through that shadowy wood where allegories
lurk unseen, we should arrive, after perhaps one day's journey, on the open plain
of moral truth."—SC 16:1; OB 1:89-90; CF 4:115. For an excellent and
comprehensive treatment of the way in which the Cistercian Fathers and
their contemporaries used the Scriptures with their four senses see H. de Lubac,
Exégèse Médiévale: Les Quatre Sens de l'Ecriture, 4 vols. (Paris: Aubier, 1959-
1964). There are many references to St Bernard in the indexes.

ten but it could have been only a matter of a few years after
the initial publication.[12] Yet already "many copies had been
made." For those times this was significant. Copies were made
only by the painstaking labors of a copyist. One did not undertake the expenditures and troubles involved in copying a book
unless there was a real demand for it. Bernard's writings, even
in his lifetime, were in great demand and widely read.[13]

Bernard would learn from his experience with the *Steps of
Humility*. In the future he would be more cautious in pub-
lishing.[14] Usually he would submit his work to friends for
their judgment.[15] He was however not always fortunate in his
choice of critics. We know now that some of the sharpest passages in his *Apologia* were not originally his own but were
inspired by one of these chosen critics.[16] We find, too, that
these critics sometimes could not resist the temptation to
"leak" the work.[17]

12. The "long after" (*multo post*) of the *Retractatio* has to be understood in
the context. It was much too late after publication for Bernard to introduce into
the text the corrections he would like to make. It does not mean necessarily that
many years had elapsed. After the publication of many more significant and
controversial works he would not have been apt to concern himself about pub-
lishing a retractation concerning relatively minor matters in this first treatise.

13. The diffusion of the mss solidly establishes this.

14. Unlike most of his works there seem to have been no successive redactions
of the treatise; the first one was published. See the Introductions in OB and CF.

15. Eg, in the case of his next treatise, the *Apologia*. He had sent it to Oger, a
Canon Regular of Mont-Saint-Eloi, and wrote to him in this vein: ". . . do not, on
any account, allow anyone to see or copy the aforesaid booklet until you have
been through it with him (William of St Thierry), discussed it with him, and have
both made such corrections as may be necessary that every word of it may be
supported by two witnesses. I leave to you both to decide whether the preface
you have put together out of my letters will stand, or whether it would not be better to compose another."—Ep 88:3; PL 182:213; tr. B. S. James, *The Letters of
St Bernard of Clairvaux* (Hereafter cited as LSB) (London: Burns and Oates, 1953),
Letter 91 (James' numbering is different from that of the PL), pp. 136f. This is
cited in Leclercq's Introduction in CF 1:7f. In his Prologue to the treatise, *On
Grace and Free Will*, Bernard wrote to William of St Thierry: "You please read it
first . . . if you notice something obscurely stated . . . do not hesitate either to
emend it yourself or else to return it to me for emendation. . . ." OB3:165, CF19.
See also two articles by Leclercq, "Les formes successives de la lettre-traité de s.
Bernard contre Abélard" in *Revue bénédictine* 78 (1968): 87-105 and "Les let-
tres de Guillaume de Saint-Thierry," *ibid.* 79 (1969): 375-391. Also, CF 1:7ff.

16. See CF 1:24f.

17. So Bernard had to write to Oger: "That other booklet I lent you, I had
meant you only to read, but you tell me that you have had it copied. . . . I did
not intend that you should send it to the abbot. . . ."—Ep 88:3, *loc. cit.*

GODFREY OF LANGRES

Like most of Bernard's works, this first one was written in response to the behest of a friend who had some title to make such a demand on the busy abbot. Besides the title of friendship, often there were other accompanying claims. In this case it was that of filiation. The *Steps of Humility* were written for Godfrey of Langres who was then abbot of Clairvaux's second foundation, Fontenay.[18]

We should know more about this man for he was perhaps the man closest to Bernard, the Abbot. For a time he was Bernard's prior, then he was sent off to head the second foundation. Soon again we find him back at Clairvaux.[19] We might well ask why? We have seen parallel instances in modern times and the reasons are various. Some men make excellent priors but poor first superiors. This may have been the case with Godfrey. But his subsequent election as Bishop of Langres in 1139 and his successful administration of that diocese for about twenty-three years would seem to indicate he had real ability to lead and govern. The reason for the return might have been the same as that which motivated his later resignation from the bishopric: a nostalgia for Clairvaux, a basic lifelong attraction to live the simple, free life of a monk. We have parallels to this, as for example in the case of the Blessed Humbert, the founding abbot of Igny, who after ten years of service, in spite of Bernard's strong disapproval, laid down his charge and returned to the ranks of Clairvaux.[20] But the real answer perhaps lay in the needs of Bernard and Clairvaux. It was a rapidly developing community. Young and old were flocking to it, foundations were going forth from it at a dis-

18. Fontenay was founded in 1119. See L. Janauschek, *Originum Cisterciensium* (Vienna: Hoelder, 1877) p. 8, where all the details are given as well as a brief biographical sketch of Godfrey.

19. There is some discussion as to when he returned to Clairvaux. Leclercq (OB 3:3), citing Vacandard (*Vie de saint Bernard, Abbé de Clairvaux* [Paris: Lecoffre, 1895] 1:166 note 4), sets his return sometime before 1126. Janauschek (*loc. cit.*) and Mills (*op. cit.* vii), citing Gallia Christiana (4:374) has him return around 1135.

20. See J. Morson and H. Costello, Introduction in Guerric of Igny, *Liturgical Sermons I,* CF 8:xvi.

turbing rate.[21] Bernard would often be off on the business of
Church and State.[22] There was need of an exceptionally capable second-in-command. Yet he would have to be very truly
a second-in-command, there was no room for undue indepen-
dence. Bernard, the genius, even with all his commitments
kept a close watch on things. Bernard, the spiritual father,
knew his sons and kept in close personal contact with each
one of them, as is evident from some of the stories that have
come down to us.[23] The prior would "perform respectfully the
duties enjoined on him by his abbot and do nothing against
the abbot's will or direction."[24]

THE YOUNG BERNARD

Whether we are reading the treatise to get better in touch
with the exciting, unusual and extremely significant period
of history during which it was written, or to get to know a
fascinating personality better, or simply to deepen our own
spiritual insight, we do well to consider the man who speaks
to us, to have a real feel for him, so that, in a sense, we can
enter into dialogue with him.[25]

Bernard of Fontaines was by origin a man of the upper classes. His family had its place among the nobility of the emerging
French nation. He was well educated. His writings give evidence
of some familiarity with the classics and an excellent training

21. In the years Godfrey would have been prior, if we accept Leclercq's date,
Clairvaux would have acquired 25 new daughter houses. In all it was to acquire
65 during Bernard's term of office. See the chart in the back of Janauschek.

22. It was during Godfrey's tenure that Bernard had among other things to strug-
gle with the papal schism which was settled just prior to Godfrey's election as
bishop, an election, incidentally, which was first given to Bernard who declined
the office

23. See J. Leclercq, "St Bernard of Clairvaux and the Contemplative Community"
in *Contemplative Community: An Interdisciplinary Symposium,* CF 21 (1972)
pp. 108-149.

24. RB 65:16.

25. Still perhaps the best biography of Bernard is that of Vacandard (cited above
in note 19) but one should not overlook the *Vita Prima* PL 185:225-416, partial
tr. G. Webb and A. Walker, *Saint Bernard of Clairvaux* [London: Mowbray, 1960]).
The most recent authoritative study on Bernard is that of Leclercq, *St Bernard and
the Cistercian Spirit,* CS 16.

in composition. He uses every literary form, is masterfully at home in all of them. In the fullest sense of the word, he is literate.

And he had extraordinary powers of leadership. When he decided Cîteaux was the right answer, he did not go alone. He led thirty relatives and friends into the marshes. He was not a naive lad, unfamiliar with the ways of the world. He pursued a married brother into a front-line army camp, he spoke frankly to uncle and brothers and friends alike. He would be well prepared and knowledgeable when he later offered advice and direction to kings and princes, bishops and clerics, knights and scholars. And he could identify with the poor.

The man who wrote the *Steps of Humility* was not humble by origin, nature or temperament. It was a virtue, he knew from experience, that had to be cultivated—and at a price. The aspirant of twenty-three (we must remember that twenty-three in those days represented a good bit more maturity than its parallel today) must have also been spiritually maturing. Otherwise it would hardly have been possible for him to have reached so rapidly that spiritual maturity which would have allowed the Abbot of Cîteaux, St Stephen Harding, to send him forth as the spiritual father of Cîteaux's third daughter house.

When Bernard wrote the *Steps of Humility* he had been abbot for about ten years. He had known the rigor of a Cistercian novitiate, made more rigorous by his own zeal, a couple of years of community life as a simple monk, and then years of ever more weighty responsibility as the abbot of a rapidly growing community. He was plagued by serious ill health. He had to travel much—much for an ordinary Cistercian abbot though not much in comparison to what the future would demand of him—seeing bishops and nobles to get the permission, backing and finances for Clairvaux's initial foundations—the first in what would be a steadily growing stream. His life had been enriched by sharing it with some wonderful friends: William of Champeaux, his bishop, William of St Thierry, who convalesced with him in the little hut in the garden, Guerric of Igny, who came to Clairvaux around 1123, a saintly scholar with years of learning and prayerful solitude behind him, and Bernard's own remarkable brothers and uncle. Though still young, only thirty-five, the Abbot of Clairvaux had a lot to draw on when he set about responding to the Abbot of Fontenay.

THE STEPS OF HUMILITY

What Bernard dictated to his secretary was not wholly new. Godfrey in making his request had in mind some conferences which he himself had heard from the lips of the abbot when he sat at his right in the chapter house at Clairvaux. Now Godfrey found himself in a center chair and he wanted to provide equally good food for the community that had been entrusted to his care.

Bernard opens with a somewhat stylized exordium. Yet it has its truth. It undoubtedly was a great act of charity for a very busy abbot to take time out to prepare these many pages for Godfrey.

THREE STEPS OF TRUTH

Bernard is a good teacher. Before constructing his steps of humility he arouses his reader's interest by showing him the heights to which they can lead. After all, who is interested in a ladder except the man who wants to climb up to something. And that something is truth, but truth taken in a very large and full sense; not just a moral habit or a quality of the mind, but the Incarnate Word, God himself known and contemplated, and that truth which in man operates by charity.

In speaking of his goal Bernard the teacher seeks a paradigm, and finds it again in steps. For him there are three steps or degrees of truth. Threefold divisions are a constant in this treatise, they occur again and again.[26]

Even before going into the three degrees of truth, Bernard

---

26. Eg: way, truth, life (1) [The numbers in parentheses refer to the paragraphs in the treatise] humility, charity, contemplation (3-5), truth, mercy, illumination (13-19), humility of the Son, love of the Spirit, light of the Father (20-1). Even the 12 steps are divided into 3 groups: despising one's brethren, one's superiors, one's God. See below note 36, p. 11.

pauses to speak of the three fruits to be gained by mounting
these steps of humility: humility itself, love and contemplation. These correspond to the three degrees of truth, or more
accurately as Bernard notes, the three degrees of perception
of truth; the truth in oneself, the truth in one's neighbor and
the Truth in itself. Bernard asserts there is a precise order here
and establishes this both by intrinsic reasons and by an appeal
to authority. His authority is Christ Jesus teaching on the
Mount, it is the Beatitudes.

Just as under the guidance of the Spirit the inspired writer
or redactor gathered in summary form the full teaching of
Christ into the three chapters of Matthew's Gospel that form
the Sermon on the Mount,[27] so the essence of that whole
sermon is distilled in the Beatitudes that stand at the head of
it. The Cistercian Fathers clearly perceived this and used this
text to trace out a Cistercian way to holiness.[28] Bernard would
do this later in his First Sermon for the Feast of All Saints.[29]
But here in this first treatise he already makes use of the Beatitudes as a sure guide for the ascent in truth. First the poor,
meek, sinner humbles himself with tears and thirsts for justice.[30] He sees himself as he truly is, with all his sin and misery.
Such a heart that knows misery, knows mercy. Thus he can
readily identify with his brother. Bernard demonstrates his
understanding of human psychology here as he declares: "A
brother who does not live in harmony with his brothers . . .
has no sympathy with them because their feelings do not affect
him, he can never really see the truth in others. . . . a brother's
miseries are truly experienced only by one who has misery in
his own heart." (6) The second degree of truth, a real understanding of others, is only attained by the merciful, and one is
merciful only when he first perceives his own misery[31]. But

27. Mt 5-7.
28. See M. B. Pennington, ' A Cistercian Way to Holiness," *Cistercian Studies* 6
(1971): 269-281.
29. OB 5:327-341; CF 34.
30. "Blessed are the poor in spirit, for theirs is the kingdom of heaven.
"Blessed are those who mourn, for they shall be comforted.
"Blessed are the meek, for they shall inherit the earth.
"Blessed are those who hunger and thirst for righteousness, for they shall
be satisfied."—Mt 5:3-6.
31. Below, 6, p. 34.

once he is merciful, he will obtain mercy, as is said in the fifth Beatitude: "Blessed are the merciful for they shall obtain mercy."[32] That mercy will purify him. Then as one clean of heart he will see God.[33] He will have reached the third degree of truth, he will know Truth in itself and go out of himself (*excessus*) in contemplation of it.

Bernard teaches all of this quite concisely but his illustrations greatly amplify the text. Christ is always his prime exemplar. It is when showing Christ becoming acquainted with infirmity that he might be merciful that Bernard goes off on his longest digression, exploring the knowledge of Christ. It is here where his memory fails him, modifying a Scripture text, with the results that the argumentation flowing from it is unfounded. The point is not central and Bernard had already given other bases for his opinion. In actual fact it is a question still debated by theologians today—the question of the growth of Christ the man through the acquisition of new knowledge. As the question is a bit off the point here, which Bernard himself admits in the text,[34] he does not have difficulty later when he must retract it. When it is merely a question of theological speculation Bernard has little difficulty in ceding a point.[35]

Besides the example of Christ he offers two others. The Psalmist also shows the humble man how to act (16), while the Pharisee shows exactly what not to do (17).

But Bernard, the contemplative, the mystic, the theologian, soars aloft to find even more lofty exemplars as he reaches into the Trinity itself and directs the reader's gaze to the op-

32. Mt 5:7.

33. "Blessed are the pure in heart, for they shall see God."—Mt 5:8.

34. No. 13, p. 41.

35. This is evident in many passages in his sermons, eg: "Whether I am right in assigning it to such a source, I leave it to you to judge. It is also for you to consider and decide whether I have correctly attributed the same kind of humility to the Savior. . . . Another question awaiting your determination is whether I am right in supposing. . . ."—SC 42:8; OB 2:38; CF 7; "Nevertheless, if you still insist . . . I shall not quarrel with your conviction. . . ."—SC 50:2; OB 2:79; CF 31; "The Fathers seem to have held divergent views on the problem. . . . But I am of the opinion that knowledge of these matters would not contribute greatly to your spiritual progress."—SC 5:7; OB 1:24; CF 4:29.

erations of the Father, Son and Holy Spirit. The Son, by word
and example, teaches humility. The Spirit pours out his com-
passionate love into the hearts of the humble. And the Father
beatifies them through Truth. They progress from disciples
to friends to sons. The Son who is Truth works in the mind,
the Spirit who is love in the will, but the Father draws men
out of themselves into ecstatic contemplation, to the third
heaven, to the attainment of the third and highest degree of
truth.[36]

TWELVE STEPS OF HUMILITY

It is the ladder of humility that gets a man up to the first
step of truth. And Bernard now finally turns his attention to
this ladder. It is not an unknown climb, for the way of humility and the way of pride are the very same. The way we
have descended by pride we must ascend by humility.

It is a good pedagogical principle that one should go from
the known to the unknown. Bernard does this using the opportunity to give further evidence of his own humility. Instead
of describing the steps of humility in themselves, he exemplifies them by their opposites, saying this is the way he knows
them best—not by climbing up the ladder, but by sliding down
it through pride.

His paradigm here is Benedict's twelve degrees or steps of
humility as they are sketched out in the seventh chapter of
his *Rule for Monasteries,* something that would be very well-

---

36. What has been said here might be summed up in schematic fashion something like this:

Person	operates in	to make	producing in them	corresponding Beatitudes
Son	intellect	disciples	humility—knowledge of self	1-4
Holy Spirit	will	friends	love, mercy—of neighbor	
Father	rapture	sons	contemplation—of God, Truth	6

known and familiar to his monastic audience. This is the Rule that was so dear to the early Cistercians, the observance of which they saw to be the very living of the Gospel.[37] It was the desire to live this Rule more perfectly that animated the Founders of Cîteaux,[38] the men who inspired and formed Bernard as a monk. Chapter seven has always been considered the heart and center of the Rule, the essence of Benedictine ascesis, the Benedictine way to perfect love.[39] It perhaps says something for the sureness of Bernard's insight into the meaning of his Cistercian vocation and the Cistercian way of life that his first treatise is concerned with the very center of the Rule. And the way he goes about it indicates something of the specific emphasis of the Cistercian spirit. For, as we have seen Bernard clearly sees, the whole value of the ladder, of Benedictine ascesis, lies in its ability to bring us to the way of truth with its culmination in ecstatic contemplation. The Cistercians are Benedictine contemplatives.

If the reading has sometimes been heavy, even laborious, in the first part of this treatise, especially when Bernard struggled with the problem of the knowledge of Christ, it now takes a

---

37. Thurston of York, speaking of the founders of Fountains, speaks of: ". . . thirteen men who were determined to correct their way of life according to the Rule of Saint Benedict, or rather, according to the truth of the Gospel." And he goes on to put these words into the mouth of the leader, Robert of Fountains: "We must undertake with all our strength to observe by God's grace the true and age-old service of our blessed Father Benedict, or rather, the more ancient Gospel of Christ. . . ." And Thurston goes on to comment: "We ought to recall what happened in the affair of the Molesme monks which is quite similar. The Cistercians went forth to establish and found a most perfect way of life. . . . They faithfully undertook a renewal of the Holy Rule and a total living of it. . . . Indeed, it is clearer than light that in their wonderful way of life the truth of the whole Gospel shines forth."—nos. 3, 4, 22; PL 182:697-704; tr. M. B. Pennington, "Three Early Documents," *Cistercian Studies* 4 (1969): 149-158.

38. This is evident throughout the *Exordium Parvum*: eg, "These men, while still living in Molesme and inspired by divine grace often spoke, complained and lamented among themselves over the transgression of the Rule of St Benedict, the Father of Monks. . . . That was the reason why they came into this solitude, namely to fulfill their vows through the observation of the Holy Rule."—c. 3, *Nomasticon Cisterciense*, ed. M. Séjalon (Solesmes: S. Pierre, 1892), p. 55; tr. R. Larkin in L. Lekai, *The White Monks* (Okauchee: Cistercians, 1953), p. 253.

39. See my article "Discerning the Spirit and Aims of the Founders of the Order of Cîteaux" in *The Cistercian Spirit: A Symposium*, CS 3:1-26, especially pp. 23ff.

lighter turn—though certainly not frivolous. It is undoubtedly this latter part with its delightful vignettes that made the treatise so popular.

The order of Bernard's treatment then is wholly determined by that of his master, Benedict. At the end of the first part he indicates precisely how his twelve descending steps of pride correspond to Benedict's twelve ascending steps of humility. Actually this is more fully presented at the head of the whole treatise where the two ladders or rather the two directions of the same ladder are presented in summary form. Whether this is the work of Bernard or a very early redactor we do not know but it is certainly part of the manuscript tradition.[40]

However even in his treatment of the twelve steps St Bernard reverts to his much favored tripartite division and shows, as an appendix to the tenth step of pride, how the first six steps show contempt for the brethren, the next four for the superiors and the last two for God. Conversely the first two steps of humility are in relation to God and it is only when a man has attained this humility will he want a superior over him and enter a monastery. Thus St Bernard argues that the last two steps of pride will be found only outside the monastery—some consolation for monks!

The reader immediately notices that Bernard's treatment of the first step of pride is as long as his treatment of the other eleven put together. This might have been forced on Bernard by external circumstances. He might have wanted to treat them all more fully, drawing abundantly on Scripture for illustrations as he does with the first, but the pressure of time or a waiting messenger or an impatient Godfrey may have forced him to hastily conclude his work.[41] But we have no evidence that this was actually the case. His reason might have been that

---

40. There is no basis for asserting they are actually Bernard's work, yet they are contemporary to him. See OB 3:9f.

41. We have an example of this occuring in the case of the *Apologia* where Bernard says: "I am prevented from going on by the burdens of my office, and by your imminent departure, dear brother Oger. You will not agree to stay any longer, and you refuse to go without this latest little book."—*Apologia* 30; OB 3: 106f; CF 1:67.

he thought this was where most of his monastic hearers were or were in the greatest danger of being. Or it may have been simply that his charismatic freedom was spurred on by the abundance of relevant Scriptural passages that sprang to mind. Certainly his long excursus on the apostate Seraph has much to do with the length. It parallels in some ways his long excursus on the knowledge of Christ found in the first part. Perhaps in this balance we have a bit of subtle artistry which we do not readily perceive or appreciate. We could also note another parallel here, certainly one unintended by the author. Of the two points treated in the *Retractatio* one is found in each of these sections. When Bernard launches out into speculation he is not only less interesting and lively but also more apt to err as he ventures to set forth his own opinions.

Since the text itself offers a summary schema of the twelve steps down and up[42] there is no need to summarize them here. After studying the schema one will want to enter simply into the reading and thoroughly enjoy the delightful illustrations with which Bernard colors his presentation. Bernard brings out clearly enough in the text how one step leads to another and how each step of pride corresponds to its relative step of humility. As we have already noted, after the tenth step he offers a brief three-part summary which is also helpful.[43]

At the conclusion of the twelfth step Bernard launches into another, perhaps more interesting, excursus, struggling with an exegetical problem. John the Evangelist has written—Bernard applies the text to the habitual sinner of the twelfth step—"For such a one I would not that anyone should pray."[44] This is a hard saying, especially for the loving heart of the abbot. He subtly undermines the text by reducing its application to expressed petition. Modern exegetes come at the problem from another approach, but Bernard has the authority of Augustine for his.[45] And it is a satisfying answer he gives, one that cor-

---

42. Below, pp. 26-27.
43. Below, pp. 75-76.
44. 1 Jn 5:16.
45. See below, p. 78, note 357.

responds to lived experience. The heart does not need words, nor can words and precepts obliterate the longings of a loving heart which God cannot fail to see.

As we finish reading the steps of pride we are inclined to expect our teacher to begin now the ascent. But a bit of reflection will make us realize that not only has he related the steps of pride to the corresponding steps of humility but in so doing he has fully instructed us in the latter. Nonetheless it is with a certain amount of disappointment that we bump into a conclusion.[46] Bernard sensed this reaction and most of the brief concluding paragraph is devoted to showing how one knowing the descending steps of pride knows at the same time the ascending steps of humility. In spite of these concluding remarks there were readers who yet felt they had been deceived in their expectation (and so might we). This is evident from the fact that Bernard had to touch again on the matter in his *Retractatio*.[47]

It might be useful to offer the reader here a schematic outline of the treatise:

Preface
A. The Goal of the Steps of Humility—Truth (doctrinal presentation
    1. The Sources
        a. Scriptural: the teaching of Christ (1)[48]
        b. Patristic: Augustine's definition of humility (2)
    2. The Goal in general—the three fruits: humility charity, contemplation (3-5)

46. I am aware that Leclercq has indicated this treatise as one where Bernard achieved a beautiful ending (J. Leclercq, "L'Art de la composition dans les traités de s. Bernard," *Recueil*, vol. 3 [1969], p. 117. This article is reprinted from *Revue bénédictine* 76 [1966]: 87-115.). I am not disagreeing with this. My "bump" is something more psychological. The treatise, even in its ending, is a beautiful masterpiece of literature.

47. "Some have objected to the title: 'The Steps of Humility,' on the grounds that I have described the steps not of humility but of pride. They must not have understood or have not noticed my note at the end where I briefly explain the title."—below, p. 25.

48. The numbers in paraenthesis refer to the paragraphs in the text.

SOURCES

One of the first things that usually strikes one when he first reads St Bernard is the copious use of Scripture. Texts flow from Bernard's pen without cease. When he is not actually quoting a text he is frequently using Biblical words and phrases to express his own ideas.

We have already mentioned the freedom Bernard takes when using Scriptural texts. He is always more intent on content. Sometimes he does argue his point from a Biblical text employing the type of tight argumentation which we are inclined to associate with the scholastic method. We find some examples of this in the opening paragraph of this treatise. Although the "last of the Fathers" spoke disparagingly of the philosophers of the schools[49] he knew the new methods and made some use of them.[50] But it is evident that it is the Fathers who have more fully informed his mind and shaped his method and style. He usually employs Scripture in the more contemplative and existential way of the patristic tradition.

In this treatise his dependence on the Fathers is extensive right from the beginning where he employs Augustine's definition of humility (2). He weaves into his fabric themes and interpretations common to the Fathers, such as the interpretation of Isaiah 14:13 and Ezekiel 28:12 (31, 35) or the theme of Eve, mother of the dying (30).

---

49. Eg, Pent 3:5 (however it is interesting to note that even in this very sermon Bernard examines his matter through what the philosophers would call the four causes, and does it in excellent philosophical form), OB 5:173, CF 25, IV 3 p.3, OB 5:203, CF 25; SC 22:10, OB 1:136, CF 7.

50. In fact we can find in the second paragraph of this treatise a perfect syllogism with its major, minor (*Sed*) and conclusion (*ergo*). See OB 3:18. This has been somewhat lost in the translation.

The Fathers who seem to have the greatest influence on him in this treatise are men of the West, Augustine and Gregory the Great, but Origin is not absent. There are also evidences of Justin, Cyprian, Tertullian, Ambrose and Anselm.[51] The works of all these Fathers, with the possible exception of Justine, were to be found in the amarium at Clairvaux.[52]

There are also quotations coming from pagan authors such as Terence (6) and Persius (40). Bernard may have remembered these from his school days, though there is greater likelihood that they came to him through the Fathers.

Obviously the primary source here is Benedict of Nursia who is responsible for the whole structure of the second part and even at times provides the very words Bernard uses.

The liturgy also provides Bernard with inspiration and content. As we have already indicated, his Scriptural texts come to him often through the liturgy. In paragraph twenty-two he employs a phrase that comes from the *Sanctus* of the Mass or the *Te Deum,* a phrase inspired by Isaiah: "The heavens and the earth are filled with your glory."[53] And one of his final arguments in the treatise rests on liturgical practice, on the way the Church prays in the prayers of the faithful on Good Friday (56).

THE STYLE OF THE TREATISE

Very much could be written about the style of St Bernard, even if one limited himself to the consideration of this initial treatise. I will touch on only a few points.[54]

One thing that is very evident is the order in the treatise. It is carefully planned and well executed. The outline offered above[55] makes this quite clear. Yet another facet of Bernard

---

51. The notes of the text should be consulted.
52. See A. Wilmart, "L'Ancienne biblithèque de Clairvaux," *Collectanea OCR* 11 (1949): 101-127, 301-319.
53. Is 6:3.
54. A fuller treatment of this matter can be found in J. Leclercq, "L'Art de la composition dans les traités de S. Bernard," *Recueil*, vol. 3 (1969), 105-162, reprinted from *Revue bénédictine* 76 (1966): 87-115.
55. Pp. 26-27.

is equally in evidence: his freedom even when working within a structure. Besides the three main excursuses which we have already indicated (7-12, 31-38, 52-56), there are a number of other instances where he has rambled down a side road. It is something of which he is frankly aware: "But to come back to our subject." (13) "I am afraid I am 'speaking in my excess' now myself and have wandered away from my subject. . . . Well let us come back to the point." (17-18) "How did we get on to this matter . . .? I wandered off into this by-path. . . ." (38).

Basically though, even with his vagaries, the author of this treatise is a good teacher. The use of the twelve steps and the very frequent use of the tripartite division are good memory aids. The interrelationship of the different parts and aspects are clearly brought out.[56] Principal terms such as humility and pride are clearly defined,[57] distinctions are neatly made.[58] Argumentation, flowing in good theological fashion from Scripture texts, is clearly pursued and brought to a conclusion.[59] Even very deep theological questions such as the properties of the three divine Persons, concomitance and attribution are handled with a simplicity and clarity that is readily intelligible to the average lay reader.[60]

However, Bernard's pedagogical style, order and clarity detract not at all from the literary value of his treatise.[61] Unfortunately much of the beauty of Bernard's Latin is not and probably can never be captured in translation. The emphasis and alliteration of *Carnalis videlicit populi sententiam de carne inquirens, nomen carnis posuit* (11) is not found in "When he was enquiring what a carnal people thought about the human

56. See above, note 36.
57. "Humility is a virtue by which a man has a low opinion of himself because he knows himself well." (2) "For what else is pride but, as a saint [Augustine] has defined it, the love of one's own excellence." (14)
58. Eg, in relation to the two kinds of excess (16-17).
59. Eg, in no. 1. See Leclercq, "L'Art. . . ." p. 114.
60. See nos. 20-22.
61. Leclercq concludes his consideration of the treatise by saying: "One finds in this treatise of Bernard *junior* a doctrinal synthesis which will lose none of its value in the face of his more mature works. But also in regards to composition this first work is already a masterpiece."—"L'Art . . ." p. 117.

body that they saw before them he used the title that referred directly to the human nature. . . ."[62] Alliteration abounds in the Latin.[63] The constant balancing of words, again often with alliteration, delights both ear and mind:

> . . . *sicut prius misericordes quam mundicordes, sic prius mites quam misericordes.* . . . (14)

> *Si non accessisset, non attraxisset; si non attraxisset, non extraxisset.* (12)

> . . . *se solum decipit, quem solum excipit.* . . . (17)

> . . . *vel de virtute confidam, vel pro labore diffidam.* (22)

> . . . *ideoque nascimur morituri, quia prius morimur nascituri.* (30)

But even in translation Bernard's skill as a writer stands out in the delightful character sketches in the second part—delightful to the reader but one suspects that they might have caused more than one monk to squirm when they were first sketched out in the chapter house at Clairvaux. Not only are they full of humor, but paint their subject with such vividness that we can immediately see and hear the loquacious eccentric braggart:

> his eyes are wandering, his glance darts right and left, his ears are cocked (28) . . . he simply cannot stop laughing. . . . He is like a well-filled bladder that has been pricked and squeezed. The air, not finding a free vent, whistles out through the little hole with squeak after squeak . . . In embarrassment he buries his face in his hands, tightens his lips, clenches his teeth. It is no use. The laughter must explode and if his hand holds it in his mouth, it bursts out through his nose. (40)
> While he is at his meal, he casts his eyes around the tables and if he sees anyone eating less than himself he is mortified. . . . He would rather starve. . . . He wonders what others think about the appearance of his face and as he

---

62. Below, p. 39.

63. Eg: *Hauris virus peritura, et perituros paritura.* (30) . . . *ut scire sciatur quod scit.* (41) . . . *miserabilius mirisque clamoribus miram misericordiam meruit.* . . . (54) *Sapere enim malum, sapere non est, sed desipere.* (30)

cannot see it he can only guess whether it is rosy or wan by looking at his hands and arms, poking at his ribs, and feeling his shoulders and loins to see how skinny or fleshy they are. . . . He will stay awake in bed and sleep in choir. After sleeping through the night office while the others were singing psalms, he stays on to pray alone. . . . He makes sure that those sitting outside know he is there, modestly hidden in his corner, clearing his throat and coughing and groaning and sighing. (42)
He must have the first place in gatherings, be the first to speak in council. He comes without being called. He interferes without being asked. He must rearrange everything, re-do whatever has been done. (44)
. . . when they[64] are caught out . . . their eyes are cast down, they humble themselves to the very dust, they will wring out some tears if they can, sighs and groans interrupt their words. . . . They accuse themselves of things so great, so incredible, that you begin to doubt the charges you were certain of before. (46)

The force of the satire is heightened by the realism of the descriptions.

The same mastery of description is to be found at work when Biblical scenes or personalities are brought in to illustrate a point.[65]

Through all this Bernard shows his depth of psychological insight. We have already noted this in the first part.[66] We see it again in the last sentence just quoted above and again as he speaks of the community's reaction when the proud hypocrite is unmasked: "Now everyone knows what he is, everyone condemns him, and they are all the more vexed because of the good opinion his fraud fooled them into holding for so long." (47)

B. R. V. Mills tells us that we have in Bernard a thinker, a theologian, a monk, a mystic and a moralist.[67] I think quite a few additional adjectives could be added to even this impressive array.

---

64. Bernard switches back and forth from the singular to the plural in his illustrations.
65. Eg, Dinah (29), Eve (30).
66. See above, p. 11.
67. *Select Treatises of S. Bernard*, pp. xvff.

THE SUBTITLES

The translation presented here is based on the critical Latin text prepared by Jean Leclercq and Henri Rochais and published in 1963 by Editiones Cistercienses in volume three of the *Sancti Bernardi opera*. In the translation the subtitles or chapter headings to be found in that edition are retained. Actually they go back to the twelfth century and probably are contemporaneous with Bernard himself.[68] They are found in most of the ancient manuscripts, the one common set with few variations; though there are some later manuscripts where they do not appear. Sometimes they are listed at the head of the whole treatise rather than inserted in the text. And in some manuscripts they are both listed and inserted in the text.[69]

Whoever inserted the titles, and he quite possibly had Bernard's approval in the matter, was more concerned with utility and clarity than with symmetry. They are far more numerous in the second part, where each step commands its own title, and also the excursus on the apostate Angel. In the first part there are, besides the heading of the Preface, only two subtitles and these are drawn from the text itself.

CONTEMPORARY SIGNIFICANCE

Perhaps one of the clearest and most concrete indications of the perduring value of this treatise is the fact that there has been sufficient demand for it to warrent constant republication in many languages. In English alone in the last fifty years there has been Barton Mills' translation, based on his own edition, published by SPCK in 1929; G. Bosworth Burch's, with its long introductory study on Bernard's epistomology, published by Harvard in 1940 and 1942 and republished by Notre Dame in 1963, and G. Webb and A. Walker's version appearing in Mowbray's Fleur de Lys Series in 1957.[70] The present is the first based on the critical edition.

68. See Leclercq, "Pour l'histoire des traités de s. Bernard," *Recueil* 2:116ff. The article is a reprint from *Analecta SOC* 15 (1959): 56-78.

69. See OB 3:5ff.

70. See the Bibliography, pp. 133-135.

The reason for this popularity is within the treatise itself. As we have seen, it is rich in humor; everyone can enjoy a bit of satire. It is perhaps the work of Bernard that is easiest to read. Again every man can find himself within it. It stoops down to the lowest sinner. But it not only stoops down, it points him toward the most sublime heights. There is hope for all.

Its attractiveness for many though, most fundamentally, lies in the fact that the author truly exemplifies what he teaches and with extraordinary literary skill conveys this effectively to the reader. The reader senses that Bernard has looked deeply into himself, knows himself and approaches the reader, his fellow man, with deep understanding and true compassion. The young Bernard has already come to love all men and in the sublime vision of man which he has seen in God he has a deeper respect and a greater appreciation for the greatness of each than most men have for themselves. As Bernard meets each on the rung of misery and pride on which he is presently lodged he does not fail to assure the poor wretch that he is not alone and that he has every reason to hope for great things. Every degree of pride has its corresponding degree of humility. If Bernard's satire is at times a bit stinging, and here we perhaps perceive some of the yet unmellowed zeal of youth, there is such good humor in it that we can enjoy it, just as the Black Monks of his time so enjoyed the *Apologia*.[71] Although he may not naturally use Bernard's terminology every man finds within himself some of the experiences Bernard so graphically depicts. What is more, he quickly identifies his own deepest longings in Bernard's description of the goal: the freedom of truth, universal love, the experience of the Transcendent God. Bernard's straight forward assurance, his calm witness that God really cares, is personally involved in man's strivings and fulfillment

71. See CF 1:21 and note 51 there. Surviving mss of the *Apologia* seem to indicate it was perhaps even more widely circulated among the Black Monks than among the White (or Grey as they were then called). This should not be too surprising since Bernard's reprimands of the Black, though stinging, were delightfully satirical; his reproofs for his own brothers were more straight from the shoulder.

is like a cool mountain breeze wafted across a placid lake into a city of feverish activity. It is immensely refreshing and offers one life and hope; it lifts eyes to the mountains and draws one out beyond the hustle to serene heights where he can perceive deeper meanings and experience true hope. Bernard very effectively communicates to his reader the invitation to glory in his infirmities for therein lies true strength and the hope of unending glory, meaning, fulfillment.

Enough has been said by way of introduction. Let the reader now proceed to the text and enjoy it to the full. For it offers him not only passing enjoyment, but, if he would have it, a way to a fuller—the fullest possible life and happiness.

M. Basil Pennington ocso

St Joseph's Abbey
Spencer, Massachusetts

RECONSIDERATION

(*Retractatio*)

IN THE COURSE OF THIS LITTLE WORK I referred
in support of one of my opinions to that passage of the
Gospels where our Lord says that he does not know the
day of the Last Judgement.[1] I quoted, as I thought, the text
and then found that it was not in the Gospel at all. I had no
intention of falsifying the text but I was depending on my
memory of the general sense of the passage and made a slip
in the words.[2] The true text simply says: "Not even the Son
knows."[3] I wrote: "Not even the Son *of Man* knows." I built
my whole argument on this phrase, resting a true opinion on
a false foundation. I discovered the mistake only long after I
had published the book and many copies had been made.[4]
There is no chance of tracing all these copies and correcting
the error so I suppose the only remedy is herewith to make
my confession.

In another place[5] I put forward an opinion about the Seraphim which I admit I never heard or read of anywhere. The
reader, however, will take notice that I was cautious enough
to use the words "I think." I simply expressed an opinion and
made no claim to support it from the Scriptures.

Some have objected to the title: "The Steps of Humility,"
on the ground that I have described the steps not of humility
but of pride. They must not have understood, or have not
noticed my note at the end where I briefly explain the title.[6]

1. See below, no. 11, p. 39.
2. We have here an explicit admission on the part of Bernard that he did in
practice quote Scripture from memory and that his quotations were not always
precise. This should be kept in mind when one is trying to identify his Scriptural
sources.
3. Mk 13:32.
4. We are not able to date the *Retractatio* but this sentence does indicate that
Bernard's writings, even this first one, received rather immediate wide distribution.
5. See below, no. 35, p. 63.
6. See below, no. 57, p. 82.

THE TWELVE STEPS OF HUMILITY

12. Always to show the humility in one's heart, in one's bearing, keeping the eyes lowered.
11. That a monk should speak few and reasonable words and with a moderate voice.
10. Not to be over-ready to laugh.
9. To keep silent till one is questioned.
8. To keep to the common rule of the monastery.
7. To believe and admit that one is less than others.
6. To confess and to believe that one is unworthy and useless for anything.
5. To confess one's sins.
4. To hold fast to patience amidst hard and rough things for the sake of obedience.
3. To submit to superiors in all obedience.
2. Not to love one's own will.
1. In the fear of God to be constantly on the watch against sin.[1]

The first two steps of humility are mounted outside the monastic life. This begins at the third step with submission to a superior.

---

1. These are essentially the twelve degrees of humility laid down by St Benedict in the seventh chapter of his Rule, but in inverse order as the numbers indicate. See *Sancti Benedicti Regula Monasteriorum*, ed. E. Manning (Westmalle: Typis Ordinis Cisterciensiorum, 1962), pp. 27-37; tr. L. J. Doyle, *St Benedict's Rule for Monasteries* (Collegeville: Liturgical Press, 1962), pp. 21-29 (Hereafter referred to as RB, with an indication of the chapter and verse. The verse numbers are taken from Manning who follows the standard established by Lentini and followed by Hanslik. There is as of yet no English version giving the verse numbers.).

THE DESCENDING STEPS OF PRIDE

1. Curiosity; when the eyes and the other senses attend to what is not one's concern.
2. Levity of mind, known by words that bespeak unreasonable joy and sadness.
3. Silly mirth, with over-much laughing.
4. Boasting and too much talking.
5. Singularity, proud esteem of one's own ways.
6. Self-assertion; believing one is holier than others.
7. Presumption: meddling with everything.
8. Defending one's sins.
9. Hypocritical confession, which can be tested by harsh reproof.
10. Rebellion against superiors and brethren.
11. Freedom in sinning.
12. The habit of sin.

The last two downward steps take place outside the cloister. In the first six steps we find contempt for the brethren; in the next four, contempt for the superior; in the last two, contempt for God.

PREFACE

YOU ASKED ME, BROTHER GODFREY,[1] to write out at greater length the sermons I gave to the brethren on the steps of humility. I should very much like to have given a worthy response such as was due to your request, but I felt some doubts about my powers so, as the Gospel advises,[2] I first sat down and reckoned up my assets to see if they were enough to bring me through the work. Charity overcame this fear.[3] Then immediately a new wave of terror swept over me from the other side. I began to fear more the terrible danger of pride if I did well than the disgrace if I did badly. There I was at a crossroad between fear and charity, not knowing which way was safe to take. If I spoke to any profit about humility I feared to be found lacking in it; if humility kept me silent I would be good for nothing. Neither course was safe; I had to take one or the other. Finally I decided it was better to send you this cargo of words than to seek safety by lying snug in the harbor of silence, feeling confident that if you find anything worth-while in what I write, you will pray that I may be saved from pride. If, on the other hand, you find nothing worth reading—which is what I expect—well, then I will have nothing about which to be proud.

1. Godfrey is a relative of St Bernard who accompanied him to Cîteaux and Clairvaux. At the time this was written he was probably the Abbot of Clairvaux's second daughter house, Fontenay. He was to return to Clairvaux as prior and later to be elected Bishop of Langres. See above, Introduction, p. 5. This first work as most of Bernard's was written in response to a particular request.

2. Lk 14:28.

3. 1 Jn 4:18.

THE GOAL OF THE STEPS OF HUMILITY

BEFORE I SPEAK of the different steps of humility—
which indeed St Benedict does not ask us to count but
to climb[1]—I will first try to show what we may expect
to find at the top. The toil will be easier if we have the profit
before our eyes. Our Lord shows us plainly both the difficulty and the reward of the work. "I am the Way, the Truth,
and the Life."[2] The way is humility, the goal is truth. The first
is the labor, the second the reward. But you may ask: "How
do I know that he is speaking of humility? He only uses a general word, 'I am the Way' "? Well, I will give you a clearer test.
"Learn of me for I am meek and humble of heart."[3] He points
to himself as an example of humility, a model of meekness.
Imitate him and you will not walk in darkness but will have
the light of life.[4] What is the light of life but truth that enlight-
ens every man that comes into this world[5] and shows us where
the true life is to be found? So, when he says: "I am the Way
and the Truth," he adds, "and the Life." It is as if he said: "I
am the Way, I lead to Truth; I am the Truth, I promise Life;
and I myself am the very Life I give you." "For this is eternal
life, that they may know you the one true God and Jesus Christ
whom you have sent."[6] Supposing, then, that you go on to
object: "I see the way—humility; I long for the goal to which
it leads—truth; but what if the way is so difficult that I can
never reach the goal?" The answer comes promptly: "I am

1. RB 7. Cf. Mor IX, 36. 3. Mt 11:29. 5. Jn 1:9.
2. Jn 14:6. 4. Jn 8:12. 6. Jn 17:3.

29

the life," that is, I am the food, the viaticum,[7] to sustain you on your journey.

There are some who go astray and cannot find the road. He cries to them: "I am the Way." Some doubt and waver in their faith. His word to them is: "I am the Truth." To those who grow weary with the climbing his cry is: "I am the Life." I think now I have dwelt long enough on this passage of the Gospel to show you that the knowledge of truth is the fruit of humility. Let us turn to another text. "I confess to you, Father of Heaven and earth, because you have hidden these things (he means, of course, the secrets of truth) from the wise and prudent (meaning the proud) and revealed them to the little ones (the humble)."[8] This shows us that truth is hidden from the proud and made known to the humble.

2. To define humility: Humility is a virtue by which a man has a low opinion of himself because he knows himself well.[9] This is the virtue that belongs to those who have set their hearts to the climb and have gone from virtue to virtue, from step to step, until they reached the highest peak of humility[10] and gazed upon truth from the watch-tower of Zion.[11] "For the Lawgiver will give a blessing."[12] This means that he who gives the law is the same who gives the blessing; he who commands humility will lead safely to the truth. Who is this lawgiver? Who but the good and sweet Lord who gives a law to those who wander from the way?[13] They wander from the way

---

7. Bernard in using the word *viaticum* here probably intends it to be taken in its Biblical sense only (Deut 15:14, Josh 9:5), as food for the journey, and is not making an allusion to Viaticum, Communion brought to the dying, even though this was a common meaning of the word at his time.

8. Mt 11:25. Cf. Jas 4:6, 1 Pet 5:5.

9. Cf Augustine, *In Johannem*, Tract 25:16; [tr J. H. Newman] *Homilies on the Gospel according to St John*, 2 vols, Library of the Fathers (Oxford: Parker, 1848), 1:393. For Bernard, humility is truth, the low opinion of self must be based on fact: "Humility is not praiseworthy when it is not in accordance with the facts."—Ep 201, to Abbot Baldwin, no. 2; LSB 259, p. 339.

10. RB 7:5. Cf. SC 34:3; CF 7.

11. Ps 83:6 (The Vulgate enumeration of the Psalms is used throughout as being that which was familiar to St Bernard.) Cf. Origin, *Selecta in Psalmos* X, 2:586; PG 12:1187ff.

12. Ps 83:8.

13. Ps 24:8.

because they have gone astray from the truth. Will they then be deserted by our sweet Lord? No, the law that this good and kind Lord gives them is the way of humility by which they can return to the knowledge of the truth. The Lord is kind but also just. Because he is kind he gives them a chance of regaining safety; but because he is also just he vindicates the law. His kindness will not let them perish; his justice will not omit to impose some punishment.[14]

II.   3. This law which points the way back to truth St Benedict sums up in twelve steps[15]. Just as the ten commandments of the Law[16] and the twofold circumcision[17]—which add up to twelve—lead to Christ, so do these twelve steps which we have to climb to come to the possession of the truth. This was the ladder which was shown to Jacob[18]—a figure of humility. Leaning on the top of the ladder the Lord looks on the sons of men with eyes of truth that deceive not and cannot be deceived to see if there is any who understands and seeks God.[19] His place at the ladder's top[20] shows us that the knowledge of truth is to be found only at the summit of humility.[21] Can you not hear him calling from his lofty station and crying to those who seek him, for he knows who are his own:[22] "Come to me all you who desire me and eat your fill of my fruits?"[23] "Come to me all you who labor and I will refresh you."[24] He says: "Come!" Where? "To me, the Truth." How? "By humility."

14. Cf. Anselm, *Cur Deus Homo* 1:12; tr. S. N. Deane, *St Anselm,* Religion of Science Library 54 (LaSalle, Ill.: Open Court, 1939), p. 203.

15. RB 7:10-66.

16. Ex 34:28.

17. Gen 17:26, Deut 30:6, Josh 5:2, Jer 4:4, Col 2:11. Cf. St Justin, *Dialogue with Trypho;* St Cyprian: ". . . the first circumcision of the flesh is made void, and the second circumcision of the spirit is promised instead."—*Treatise XII: Three Books of Testimonies against the Jews* 1:8; tr. E. Wallis, *Ante-Nicene Fathers* (New York:Scribners, 1903), 5:510.

18. Gen 28:12; RB 7:6.

19. Ps 13:2.

20. Gen 28:13.

21. RB 7:5.

22. 2 Tim 2:19; Jn 10:14.

23. Sir 24:26.

24. Mt 11:28.

For what? "And I will refresh you." What is this refreshment which Truth promises to those who climb and gives when they gain the top? Is it perhaps love itself?[25] To this, St Benedict says, the monk will quickly come when he has climbed all the steps of humility.[26] Love is indeed a sweet and pleasant food. It refreshes the weary, strengthens the weak,[27] cheers the depressed, makes sweet Truth's yoke and light its burden.[28]

4. Love is the excellent food. Its place is in the middle of the dish of Solomon,[29] the dish which diffuses the mingled odor of the virtues, fragrant as all the powders of the perfumer.[30] It fills the hungry, and gives joy to those being filled. On this dish we find peace and patience and longanimity[31] and joy in the Holy Spirit,[32] and any other kind of virtue, any other fruit of wisdom you can think of. Humility has its own contribution to the banquet and graces the dish with the bread of sorrow[33] and the wine of compunction.[34] Truth offers these first to beginners, saying: "Rise up after you have been seated, you who eat the bread of sorrow."[35] Contemplation then brings its offering—the solid bread[36] of wisdom made of

25. "Love" in this translation generally stands for *caritas*, which denotes more a habit, a willed choice, rather than *amor*, with its more affective connotations. Where *amor* is meant this will be indicated in the notes.

26. RB 7:67.

27. Is 35:3.

28. Mt 11:30.

29. Song 3:9f. "The word *ferculum* occurs only once in the Vulgate, and means a thing on which something is carried. Thus it is taken as either 'a litter' or 'a platter.' Bernard takes it in its second meaning, and on this he bases his exhortation for us to partake in the feast of charity, whereas Gilbert of Hoyland [or Gilbert of Swineshead, *On the Song of Songs* 17:1-3; PL 184:87-89; tr. T. Berkeley, CF 13] who continued Bernard's sermons on the Song of Songs, takes it as meaning litter." —G. Webb and A. Walker, Introduction, in St Bernard, *Steps of Humility* (London: Mowbray, 1957), p. 9. They perhaps are following B. R. V. Mills, *Select Treatises of St Bernard of Clairvaux*, "De Gradibus Humilitatis et Superbiae," (Cambridge University Press, 1926), p. 83, note.

30. Song 3:6.

31. Gal 5:22.

32. Rom 14:17.

33. Ps 126:2.

34. Ps 59:5.

35. Ps 126:2.

36. Heb 5:14.

the finest wheat[37] and the wine which gladdens the heart of man,[38] to which Truth calls the perfect with the words: "Eat, my friends, and drink; be inebriated, my dearest ones."[39] Truth does not fail to make provision for the less perfect. "Love is placed in the middle for the daughters of Jerusalem."[40] These are the ones not yet able to take solid food, so Truth gives them love's milk instead of bread, and oil instead of wine. This portion is "in the middle," because beginners could not yet relish it, being too much afraid; the perfect find it insufficient now that they have plenty of the sweet food of contemplation. Beginners are not able to enjoy the sweetness of milk until they have been purged by the bitter draught of fear. It must cleanse them of the infection of carnal pleasures. The perfect now turn from milk since they have had a glorious foretaste of the feast of glory. Only those in the middle, those who are growing, who are still delicate, are content with the sweet milkfoods of charity.[41]

5. The first food, then, is humility: bitter but medicinal; the second is charity: sweet and soothing; the third is contemplation: solid and strength-giving. Lord God of Hosts, how long will you be angry with the prayer of your servant? How long will you feed me with the bread of weeping and give me tears for my drink?[42] Who will invite me to the middle banquet of the sweet food of charity where the just rejoice in the presence of God and exult for joy?[43] Then no longer will I speak

37. Ps 147:14.
38. Ps 103:15.
39. Song 5:1. Bernard explains this text more fully, outlining the three degrees of contemplation indicated by eating, drinking and inebriation in Div 87:4; OB 6-1:331f.
40. Song 3:10.
41. Bernard here introduces the classical three stages of spiritual growth: beginners, proficients and the perfect. It is in common use among the early Cistercians, forming the basic framework for William of St Thierry's *Golden Epistle* (CF 12). See J. M. Déchanet, Introduction in William of St Thierry, *Exposition on the Song of Songs*, CF 6, pp. xxxi ff and the notes there, Exp 13ff, CF 6:11ff; J. Morson and H. Costello, Introduction in Guerric of Igny, *Liturgical Sermons*, vol 1, CF 8 pp. xlix ff; M. B. Pennington, "Three Stages of Spiritual Growth according to St Bernard," *Studia Monastica* 11 (1969): 315-326.
42. Ps 79:5f.
43. Ps 67:4.

in the bitterness of my soul, saying to God: "Do not condemn me,"[44] but feasting on the unleavened bread of sincerity and truth[45] I will sing a glad song as I go in the ways of the Lord, for great is his glory.[46] Yes the path of humility is a good path.[47] It seeks for truth; it wins charity; it shares the fruits of wisdom. Just as the end of the Law is Christ,[48] so the perfection of humility is the knowledge of truth. When Christ came he brought grace; when truth is known it brings love. It is to the humble it is known. "He gives his grace to the humble."[49]

III. 6. I have now shown to the best of my powers what fruits we win by climbing the steps of humility. Now let us see if I can show how they lead to the promised reward of truth.

HOW THE STEPS OF HUMILITY LEAD TO THE PROMISED REWARD OF TRUTH

There are three degrees in the perception of truth. I will first explain these as well as I can and then we will be able to see how the twelve degrees of humility lead to these three degrees of truth. We must look for truth in ourselves; in our neighbors; in itself. We look for truth in ourselves when we judge ourselves;[50] in our neighbors when we have sympathy for their sufferings;[51] in itself when we contemplate it with a clean heart.[52] It is important to observe the order of these degrees as well as their number. First of all, truth teaches us that we must look for it in our neighbors before we seek it in itself. You will then see easily why you must seek it in yourself before you seek it in your neighbors. In the list of the beatitudes the merciful are spoken of before the clean of heart.[53] The merciful quickly grasp the truth in their neighbors when their heart goes out to them with a love that unites them so closely that they feel the neighbors' good and ill as if it were their own. With the weak they are weak, with the scandalized they

44. Job 10:1f.
45. 1 Cor 5:8.
46. Ps 137:5.
47. Ps 118:71.
48. Rom 10:4.

49. 1 Pet 5:5.
50. 1 Cor 11:31.
51. 1 Cor 12:26.
52. Mt 5:8.
53. Mt 5:7-8.

are on fire.[54] They "rejoice with those who rejoice and weep with those weep."[55] Their hearts are made more clear-sighted by love[56] and they experience the delight of contemplating truth, not now in others but in itself, and for love of it they bear their neighbors' sorrows. A man who does not live in harmony with his brothers, who mocks at those who weep and sneers at those who are glad, has no sympathy with them because their feelings do not affect him, he can never really see the truth in others. The proverb fits him well: the sound man feels not the sick man's pains, nor the well-fed man the pangs of the hungry.[57] It is fellow-sufferers that readily feel compassion for the sick and the hungry. For just as pure truth is seen only by the pure of heart, so also a brother's miseries are truly experienced only by one who has misery in his own heart. You will never have real mercy for the failings of another until you know and realize that you have the same failings in your soul. Our Savior has given us the example. He willed to suffer so that he might know compassion;[58] to learn mercy he shared our misery. It is written: "He learned obedience from the things he suffered;"[59] and he learned mercy in the same way. I do not mean that he did not know how to be merciful before; his mercy is from eternity to eternity;[60] but what in his divine nature he knows from all eternity he learned by experience in time.

7. You may not be ready to agree with me when I say that Christ the Wisdom of God[61] *learned* mercy, as if he through whom all things were made[62] could ever have been ignorant of anything that exists. This especially so since the text I quoted from the Epistle to the Hebrews can reasonably be

54. 2 Cor 11:29.
55. Rom 12:15.
56. Cf. Conv 30; OB 4:106; CF 43.
57. The first part of this proverb can be found in Terence, *Andria*, 309; otherwise its source has not been identified.
58. Heb 2:17.
59. Heb 5:8.
60. Ps 102:17.
61. 1 Cor 1:24. Bernard goes off here into an excursus (7-12) on the knowledge of Christ. He presents the alternate views held by the Fathers (See, e.g., St Anselm, *Cur Deus Homo*, 1:9; *tr. cit.*, p. 194), opts strongly for a particular one and offers a substantiating argument employing a faulty Scripture text (11) which he later has to retract (see above, p. 25).
62. Jn 1:3.

taken in another sense. It could be taken that the subject of "learned" is our Head, not in person but in his body, the Church.[63] "He learned obedience from the things he suffered" would then mean that the body learned obedience from the things our Head suffered. The death, the cross, the insults, spitting and scourging suffered by Christ give a perfect example of obedience to us his body.

St Paul says: "Christ became obedient to the Father even unto death."[64] Why had he to do that? St Peter tell us: "Christ suffered for us, leaving you an example that you might follow in his steps,"[65] by imitating his obedience. From those things which he suffered we mere men may learn how much we should be ready to suffer for obedience since for it he who himself is God did not hesitate to die. You argue then that if we take this meaning there is no difficulty about saying that Christ learned obedience or learned anything else so long as this is confined to his body, holding firmly that in his own person he could never have been ignorant of anything that happened in time; still, as Head and Body are one Christ, it is correct to say that Christ both taught and learned.

8. I will not say that you are wrong in this, but there is another text in the same Epistle which seems rather to bear out the first interpretation: "He did not lay hold on the angels, but on the seed of Abraham he laid hold; whence it was fitting that he should become like to his brothers in all things, that he might become merciful."[66] It seems to me that these words refer to the Head and could not possibly apply to the body. It is certainly about the Word of God that it is said: "He did not lay hold of the angels," meaning that he never assumed an angelic nature, but that of the seed of Abraham. We do not read that the Word was made angel, but that "the Word was made flesh."[67] and that flesh was the flesh of Abraham according to the promise made beforehand.[68] In the assuming of our nature "it behoved him in all things to be made like his brethren;" it was right and even necessary that he should be like us, subject to suffering, and experience all our miseries,

63. Col 1:24.
64. Phil 2:8; RB 7:34.
65. 1 Pet 2:21.
66. Heb 2:16-17.
67. Jn 1:14.
68. Gen 17:7; Gal 3:29.

except sin.[69] If you ask: "Why should it be necessary?" I answer: "So that he might become merciful." You object that this could apply quite well to his body. But notice the words that follow: "Because he himself has suffered and been tempted, he is able to help those who are tempted."[70] I do not see what better meaning you can draw from these words than that being like his brethren in all things means that he willed to suffer and be tempted and share in all human miseries except sin so that having thus suffered and been tempted he might learn by experience the lesson of sympathy and mercy.

9. I do not say that he became wiser by such experience, but he was seen as closer to men. And the frail sons of Adam, to whom he was willing to give the title and the reality of being brothers,[71] would have less hesitation about laying their weaknesses before him, who as God could heal them, as one close would heal them, and as one who had suffered the same would understand. For this reason Isaiah calls him "a man of sorrows and aquainted with infirmity,"[72] and the Apostle tells us: "We have not a High Priest who is unable to sympathize with our weakness."[73] Then to show from where this arises, he adds: "One who in every respect has been tempted as we are but without sinning."[74] The blessed God, the blessed Son of God, in that form in which he did not think it robbery to be equal with the Father,[75] was without doubt impassible before he emptied himself taking on the form of a slave.[76] Thus he had no experience of misery and subjection, he did not know by experience mercy and obedience. He knew by the knowledge natural to him, but not by experience. He assumed a state that was not only less than what is his by right, but even a little less than that of the angels;[77] for they too are impassible, but by grace, not by nature.[78] Lower still he came to take our form in which he could do what he could not do before, suffer and

---

69. Heb 2:16.
70. Heb 2:18.
71. Heb 2:11.
72. Is 53:3.
73. Heb 4:15.

74. *Ibid.*
75. Phil 2:6.
76. Phil 2:7.
77. Heb 2:9; Ps 8:6.

78. Bernard expresses the same opinion in Csi 5:7; OB 3:471; CF 37.

be subject to authority and learn by experience the mercy of a fellow-sufferer and the obedience of a fellow-subject. As I said already, he did not increase his personal knowledge but he deepened our trust in him when we see him from whom we strayed draw near to us to know our misery by a shared experience.[79] Hardly could we have dared to approach him in his eternal tranquility but now the Apostle can urge us to go with confidence to the throne of grace[80] because, as he tells us in another place, he has borne our weakness and our sorrows[81] and will have compassion on us since he has borne the like.[82]

10. Therefore it ought not seem absurd if it is said not that Christ began to know for the first time something which he did not know before, but that there is no contradiction in saying that something he knew from all eternity by his divine knowledge he now began in time to learn by human experience.[83] I think you will find our Lord, speaking in a similar vein when, in answer to a question of his disciples, he said that he did not know the time of the last judgment.[84] He could not be ignorant of it because in him are hidden all the treasures of wisdom and knowledge.[85] Why did he deny knowledge he must have had? It is out of the question that he could have told a lie, even to conceal from them something they had no need to know. He is wisdom and could not be ignorant; he is truth and cannot lie; he wished to stop the idle curiosity of his disciples. He replied that he did not know the thing about which they asked. He did not say absolutely that he was ignorant of it. His words allowed for a certain degree or kind of ignorance which made it true in one sense to say that he did not know. His divine gaze was upon all things, past, present and future, and saw that day clearly; but he could not experience it by any of his bodily senses. If it did come before

79. Cf. Eph 2:13.
80. Heb 4:16.
81. Is 53:4.
82. Heb 2:18; 4:15.
83. Cf. Miss 2:10; OB 4:28; CF 43.
84. Mk 18:32.
85. Col 2:3.

his bodily senses we should have to conclude that he already slew Antichrist with the breath of his mouth,[86] his bodily ears heard the sound of the trumpet-blast of the Archangel calling the dead to rise, and his bodily eyes already distinguished the sheep from the goats.[87]

11. To make it quite clear that his denial of knowledge of the last day concerned only what he knew by his bodily senses, he used carefully chosen words. He did not simply say: "I do not know;" but: "Not even the Son of Man knows."[88] The term "Son of Man" refers to the assumed human nature. When he says that there is something he does not know and uses this expression, he indicates that he is speaking as man, not as God. When he is referring to his divinity he does not say "Son" or "Son of Man," but "I" or "Me." We have several instances of this. For example, he said: "Amen, Amen, I say to you, before Abraham was made I am."[89] Note: "I am;" not: "The Son of Man is." He is clearly speaking here of his divine nature which is before Abraham and knows no beginning, not of his human nature which was born of Abraham and came into being after him. On another occasion he asked his disciples what men thought about him. "Whom do men say that the Son of Man is?"[90] In this case he did not say "I" but "the Son of Man." He changed the phrase when he was asking them about their own opinion. "Whom do you say that I am?"[91] When he was enquiring what a carnal people thought about the human body that they saw before them he used the title that referred directly to the human nature: "Son of Man." When he questioned his disciples, spiritually minded men, about his Divine Person he did not say, "Son of Man," but pointedly said "I." St Peter understood the question as we can see from his answer: "You are Christ, the Son of God."[92] If he had said:

---

86. 2 Thess 2:8.
87. Mt 25:32.
88. Mk 13:32. See above, Retractation, p. 25, where Bernard withdraws this misquotation and the argument following it.
89. Jn 8:58.
90. Mt 16:13.
91. Mt 16:15.
92. Mt 16:16.

"You are Jesus, the Son of the Virgin," he would, of course, have spoken correctly, but he was quick to notice the significance of the changed form of the question, so he aptly and properly answered: "You are Christ, the Son of God."

12. You see, then, that Christ in his one Person has two natures, one eternal, the other beginning in time.[93] According to one he knows all things eternally; according to the other there are many things he first experienced in course of time. There need then be no hesitation in admitting that, as his human nature had its beginning in time,[94] his humanly acquired knowledge of the miseries of this life had its beginning in the experience of the limitations of human nature. Our first parent, and future, and saw that day clearly; but he could not of knowledge which they could gain only by folly and woe. But their Creator,[96] seeking what was lost, followed the work of his hands and came down in mercy to where they lay in misery.[97] He would experience for himself what they rightly suffered for their disobedience. He was not led by curiosity as they were, but by a wondrous charity. It was not his intention to remain with them in misery, but to raise them from it by his mercy.

When I say he became merciful I am not speaking of the mercy that was his in the happiness of eternity; but of the mercy that sprang from sharing in our misery. The work of his tender love had its beginning in his eternal mercy, its completion in the mercy shown in his humanity. All could have been done by the eternal mercy but it would have failed somewhat in satisfying us. Both kinds of mercy were needed but the latter is more in harmony with our condition. It was conceived

93. Bernard treats of the unity of Christ more fully and formally in Csi 5:20; OB 3:483f; CF 19.

94. Rom 1:3.

95. *Protoplasti*: This word is not a biblical term but is from the Patristic tradition (eg, Tertullian, *De exhortatione castitatis* 2; PL 2:916; tr. S. Thelwall, *Ante-Nicene Fathers* [New York: Scribners, 1899], 4:51; St Cyprian, *De habitu virginis* 4; PL 4:444; tr. W. LeSaint, Ancient Christian Writers 13 [Westminster: Newman, 1951], p. 44).

96. *Plasmator*: the corresponding term to *protoplasti*, found also in Tertullian, *Adversus Judaeos* 2; PL 2:599.

97. Ezek 34:16.

with the delicacy of supreme tenderness. Could we have even imagined the infinite mercy if we had not seen it springing from one who shared our misery? In the impassibility of eternity he had an infinite compassion for us but we could never have fully realized it except for the Passion we saw him suffering. All the same if he had not first that mercy, which knows nothing of misery, he would not have come by that to which misery gives birth. If he had not that, he would not have attracted us to himself; and if he had not attracted us he would not have extracted us from the morass of misery and the slough of sin.[98] He did not lose anything of his eternal mercy but he added a new note to it; he did not change it but he multiplied it; as the Scripture says: "Men and beasts you will save O Lord: how you have multiplied your mercy O God."[99]

IV. 13. But, to come back to our subject: if he submitted himself to human misery so that he might not simply know of it, but experience it as well, how much more ought you not make any change in your condition, but pay attention to what you are, because you are truly full of misery. This is the only way, if you are to learn to be merciful. If you have eyes for the shortcomings of your neighbor and not for your own, no feeling of mercy will arise in you but rather indignation. You will be more ready to judge than to help, to crush in the spirit of anger than to instruct in the spirit of gentleness. "You who are spiritual, instruct such a one in the spirit of gentleness," says the Apostle.[100] His counsel, or better, his precept, is that you should treat an ailing brother with the spirit of gentleness with which you would like to be treated yourself in your weakness. He shows then how to find out the right way to apply this spirit of gentleness: "Considering yourself lest you also be tempted."[101]

14. It is worth noticing how closely the Disciple of Truth follows the order of his Master's thoughts. In the Beatitudes, just as the merciful, as I have said,[102] come before the clean

98. Ps 39:3.
99. Ps 35:7f.
100. Gal 6:1.

101. *Ibid.*
102. Above, no. 6, p. 34.

of heart, so the meek are spoken of before the merciful.[103] When the Apostle tells the spiritually minded to instruct the earthly minded he adds: "In the spirit of meekness."[104] The only ones who can instruct the brethren are those who are merciful, those who are meek or humble. In other words, one cannot really be merciful if he is not humble. Thus the Apostle clearly shows what I promised to prove to you, namely that we must look for truth first in ourselves, and afterwards in our neighbor. "Considering yourself," he says, that is, considering how easily you are tempted and how prone to sin, you will become meek and ready to help others in the "spirit of gentleness." If the words of the Disciple do not impress you enough, perhaps you will take warning from the stern words of the Master: "Hypocrite, first cast the beam from your own eye and then you will see better to cast the mote from you brother's."[105] The heavy, thick beam in the eye is pride of heart. It is big but not strong, swollen, not solid. It blinds the eye of the mind and blots out the truth. While it is there you cannot see yourself as you really are, or even the ideal of what you could be, but what you would like to be, this you think you are or hope to be. For what else is pride but, as a saint has defined it, the love of one's own excellence.[106] We may define humility as the opposite: contempt of one's own excellence. Neither love nor hate will give an impartial judgment. Truth will judge thus: "As I hear so I judge,"[107] not: "as I hate," nor "as I love," nor "as I fear." Hate gave its judgment: "We have a Law and according to the Law he ought to die."[108] Fear spoke: "If we let him alone, the Romans will come and take away our place and nation."[109] And we have an example of judgment swayed

103. Mt 5:4-8.
104. Gal 6:1.
105. Mt 7:5.
106. St Augustine, *Sermon* 354:6; PL 36:1565; *De Genesi ad litteram* XI, xiv, 18; PL 34:436. Bernard gives the same definition in Mor 19 (PL 182:821), adding further distinctions. In Div 47 (OB 6-1:267; CF 46) he gives a similar definition, distinguishing pride in the heart from pride in speech, pride in actions and pride in clothing.
107. Jn 5:30.
108. Jn 19:7.
109. Jn 11:48.

by love when David said of his parricide son: "Spare the boy
Absolom."[110] I understand that it is the practice in both ecclesiastical and civil courts, in accord with the law, to forbid
special friends of litigants to try their cases, lest love of their
friends blind the judges or tempt them to act unfairly.[111] If
love can make you blind or too lenient in regard to the faults
of a friend, what will your self-love do when you consider
your own faults?

15. If a man wants to know the full truth about himself he
will have to get rid of the beam of pride which blocks out
the light from his eye,[112] and then set up in his heart a ladder
of humility so that he can search into himself. When he has
climbed its twelve rungs he will then stand on the first step
of truth. When he has seen the truth about himself, or better,
when he has seen himself in truth, he will be able to say: "I
believed, therefore I have spoken; but I have been exceedingly
humbled."[113] Such a man has come to a deep heart[114] and
truth is exalted. When he reaches the second step he will say
in ecstacy: "Every man is a liar."[115] This must have been the
course that David trod. He experienced what was experienced
by our Lord and by the Apostle, what we experience ourselves by their help and example. "I believed" he says; that
means that he believed the words of Truth: "He who follows me
will not walk in darkness;"[116] "I believed (and followed him) and
therefore have I spoken"—to confess. To confess the truth
which has been believed. After believing unto justice and
speaking unto salvation "I have been humbled exceedingly,"[117]
—that is perfectly. It is as if he said: Because I have not been
ashamed to confess the known truth about myself, I have
attained to the perfection of humility. We can take *exceed-*

110. 2 Sam 18:5.
111. This provision found in all juridical codes is retained in present Church
Law, *Codex Iuris Canonici*, canon 1613. Bernard would have been familiar with it
in the Codex (AD 529) and Digest (AD 534) of Justinian.
112. Mt 7:5.
113. Ps 115:10.
114. Ps 63:7.
115. Ps 115:11.
116. Jn 8:12.
117. Jas 2:23.

ingly (*nimis*) here to mean *perfectly* as in that other text: "In his commands he takes delight exceedingly."[118] Some commentators would have it that "exceedingly" does not here mean "perfectly" but simply "very much."[119] Even so, this fits the meaning of the Prophet well enough. We can think of him as saying: When as yet I did not fully know the truth, I thought myself something, whereas I was nothing.[120] But when I had come to know Christ, to imitate his humility, I saw the truth and exalted it in me by my confession, but "I myself was humbled exceedingly,"[121] in my own eyes, I fell very low.

V. 16. The Psalmist has been humbled and now stands on the first step of truth. As he says in another psalm: "In your truth you have humbled me."[122] Up to this he has been examining himself. Now he looks out from himself to others and thus passes to the second step of truth, exclaiming in his excess: "Every man is a liar." What is meant by "in his excess?"[123] It means that he was carried away by feelings of mercy and compassion. What did he mean? He meant that every man is unreliable because too weak, helpless, and infirm to save either himself or others. It is in the same sense that the Psalmist says that "the horse is a deceptive hope of safety."[124] The horse does not deceive anyone, but a man deceives himself when he trusts too much to the horse's strength. That is what is meant by saying that "every man is a liar." He is fragile and fickle and hope in him is deceptive either for himself or for others. Indeed, there is a "curse on the man who puts his trust in man."[125] So the humble Prophet is led along his way by truth. He grieved at what he found in himself. He now sees the like in others. Sorrow and truth mount

118. Ps 111:1.
119. One such commentator would be St Anselm, *Commentary on Psalm 111*; PL 116:584. See also Bede, *De Orthographia*, PL 90:139.
120. Gal 6:3.
121. Ps 115:10.
122. Ps 118:75.
123. Ps 115:10. Bernard indicates another sense in which "excess" can be taken in the next par. when he speaks of the "excesses" of the Pharisees.
124. Ps 32:17.   125. Jer 17:5.

up together in him[126] and he burst out into the sweeping but true statement: "Every man is a liar."

17. This is very different from the conceit of the proud Pharisee. You remember the words he spoke "in his excess": "I give you thanks, O God, that I am not like the rest of men."[127] He had admiration for himself alone, for others only insults. That was not how David spoke. His words were: "Every man is a liar." He excepted no man. He did not try to deceive anyone, because he knew that "all have sinned and need the glory of God."[128] The Pharisee damned all others, excepting only himself, and fooling only himself. The Prophet shared the common mercy because he included himself in the common misery. The Pharisee waved aside mercy when he denied his misery. The Prophet said of everyone, including himself: "Every man is a liar." The Pharisee spoke of everyone except himself: "I am not like the rest of men." He gave thanks, not that he was good but that he was peerless. His gratitude was inspired not by any good he saw in himself but by the evil he saw in others. He has not yet taken the beam from his own eye but is busy counting the motes in his brothers' eyes[129]— "unjust, robbers."[130] I am afraid I am "speaking in my excess" now myself and have wandered away from my subject. Still, no harm is done if I have conveyed to you the difference between the two kinds of "excess."

18. Well! let us come back to the point. When in the light of Truth men know themselves and so think less of themselves it will certainly follow that what they loved before will now become bitter to them. They are brought face to face with themselves and blush at what they see. Their present state is no pleasure to them. They aspire to something better and at the same time realize how little they can rely on themselves to achieve it. It hurts them and they find some relief in judging themselves severely. Love of truth makes them hunger and

---

126. Eccles 1:18.
127. Lk 18:11. Cf. Ann 3:10; OB 5:41f; CF 22.
128. Rom 3:23.
129. Mt 7:5.
130. Lk 18:11.

thirst after justice[131] and conceive a deep contempt for themselves. They are anxious to exact from themselves full satisfaction and real amendment. They admit that to make satisfaction is beyond their own powers—when they have done all that is commanded them they acknowledge that they are still unprofitable servants.[132] They fly from justice to mercy, by the road Truth shows them: "Blessed are the merciful for they shall obtain mercy."[133] They look beyond their own needs to the needs of their neighbors and from the things they themselves have suffered they learn compassion: they have come to the second degree of truth.

VI.   19. If they persevere in these things: sorrow of repentance, desire for justice and works of mercy, they will cleanse their hearts from the three impediments of ignorance, weakness and jealousy and will come through contemplation to the third degree of truth. There are ways that seem good to men, [134] to the kind of men, I mean, who rejoice when they do ill and exult in evil things, and make excuses for their sins.[135] They try to hide behind the plea of weakness and ignorance.[136] They had better not flatter themselves. The excuse of ignorance and weakness will not avail if they remain deliberately weak and ignorant so as to sin more freely. It did not do much good for the first man to plead that he was not acting with full freedom because he was led astray by his wife, that is, through the weakness of the flesh.[137] Were those who stoned the first martyr, because they stopped their ears, excused by their ignorance?[138] When men realize how far they have fallen away from truth by a strong love for sin their remedy is to put that strength into their repentance and turn that love of sin into contrition. They have been weighed down by weak-

131. Mt 5:6.
132. Lk 17:10.
133. Mt 5:7. Cf. Conv 29; OB 4:104f; CF 43.
134. Prov 14:12; 16:25.
135. Prov 2:14.
136. Ps 140:4.
137. Gen 3:12ff.
138. Acts 7:57.

ness and ignorance, but weakness can be consumed in a burning desire for justice and ignorance can be dispelled by generosity. If they now ignore Truth, needy, naked and unimpressive, all too late they will blush to see Truth come in might and power with terror and reproach.[139] It will then be in vain for them to say trembling: "When did we see you in need and did not help you?"[140] Then indeed they will know the Lord when he comes to do judgment,[141] though now they choose to ignore him when he pleads for mercy. Then they will look on him whom they have pierced[142] and whom they have spurned in their greed. Now is the time to clear the eyes of the heart of every speck of weakness, ignorance and jealousy by weeping, zeal for justice[143] and perseverance in works of mercy and then to those purified eyes the promise of Truth will be fulfilled: "Blessed are the clean of heart for they shall see God."[144] These are the three steps of truth. We climb to the first by the toil of humility, to the second by a deep feeling of compassion, and to the third by the ecstacy of contemplation. On the first step we experience the severity of truth, on the second its tenderness, on the third its purity. Reason brings us to the first as we judge ourselves; compassion brings us to the second when we have mercy on others; on the third the purity of truth sweeps us up to the sight of things invisible.

VII. 20. It occurs to me here that it is possible to allot each of these three works to one of the Persons of the Undivided Trinity, that is, in so far as a man still sitting in darkness[145] can make distinction in the work of the Three Persons who always work as One. There would seem to be something characteristic of the Son in the first stage, of the Holy Spirit in the second, of the Father in the third. What is the work of the Son? "If I, your Lord and Master have washed your

---

139. Lk 21:27; Mt 24:30.
140. Mt 25:44.
141. Ps 9:17.
142. Jn 19:37.

143. Mt 5:6.
144. Mt 5:8.
145. Lk 1:79.

feet, how much more ought you also to wash another's feet."[146] The Master of truth gave his disciples an example[147] of humility and opened to them the first stage of truth. Then the work of the Holy Spirit: "Charity is spread abroad in our hearts by the Holy Spirit who is given to us."[148] Charity is a gift of the Holy Spirit.[149] By it those who, under the instruction of the Son were led to the first step of truth through humility, now under the guidance of the Holy Spirit reach the second stage through compassion for their neighbor. Finally, listen to what is said of the Father: "Blessed are you, Simon son of Jona, for flesh and blood have not revealed it to you, but my Father who is in heaven."[150] Again: "The Father will make known the truth to the sons;"[151] and, "I confess to you Father, for you have hidden these things from the wise and made them known to little ones."[152] You see: by word and example the Son first teaches men humility; then the Spirit pours out his charity upon those whom the Father receives finally into glory. The Son makes them his disciples; the Spirit consoles them as friends; the Father bestows on them the glory of sons. However, Truth is the proper title, not of the Son alone but of the Spirit and the Father too, so that it must be made quite clear, while giving full acknowledgment to the properties[153] of Persons that it is the one Truth who works at all these stages: in the first teaching as a Master, in the second consoling as a Friend and Brother, in the third embracing as a Father.

21. The Son of God, the Word and Wisdom of the Father,

---

146. Jn 13:14. Bernard adds "how much more" (*quanto magis*), perhaps in this following Ambrose, *The Mysteries* 6:33; PL 16:417, tr. R. Deferrari, in St Ambrose, *Theological and Dogmatic Works,* Fathers of the Church 44 (Washington: Catholic University, 1963), p. 17; *On Virginity,* 10:57; PL 16:294.

147. Jn 13:15.

148. Rom 5:5.

149. Acts 2:38.

150. Mt 16:17.

151. Is 38:19.

152. Mt 11:25.

153. *Proprietas*: the usual word employed by the Fathers to note those characteristics which are proper to each of the three Divine Persons; cf. Csi 5:18; OB 3:482; CF 19.

mercifully assumed to himself human reason, the first of our powers. He found it oppressed by the flesh,[154] held captive by sin, blinded by ignorance, distracted by outward things.[155] He raised it by his might, taught it by his wisdom, drew it to things interior. More wonderfully still, he delegated to it his own power of Judge. To judge is the proper act of Truth and in this it shared when out of reverence for the Word to which it is joined it became accuser, witness and judge against itself. Humility had been born from the union of the Word with human reason. Then the Holy Spirit lovingly visited the second power, the will; he found it rotten with the infection of the flesh, but already judged by reason. Gently he cleansed it, made it burn with affection, made it merciful until, like a skin made pliable with oil it would spread abroad the heavenly oil of love even to its enemies. The union of the Holy Spirit with the human will give birth to charity. See now this perfect soul, its two powers, the reason and the will, without spot or wrinkle, the reason instructed by the Word of Truth,[156] the will inflamed by Truth's Spirit;[157] sprinkled with the hyssop of humility,[158] fired with the flame of charity; cleansed from spot by humility, smoothed of wrinkle by charity;[159] the reason never shrinking from the truth, the will never striving against reason;[160] and this blessed soul the Father binds[161] to himself as his own glorious bride. Now the reason is no longer preoccupied with itself and the will is no longer concerned with other men; for this blessed soul all is lost in one delight: "The King has led me into his chamber."[162] She had become

154. Wis 9:15. See Pre 59; OB 3:292; CF 1:148; Asc 3:1; OB 5:131; CF 25.

155. Cf. Div 45:2; OB 6-1:263; CF 46.

156. 2 Cor 6:7.

157. 1 Jn 4:6.

158. Ps 50:9.

159. Eph 5:27.

160. Reason and will are meant to work freely together: Gra 4; OB 3:148: CF 19.

161. *Conglutinat*: a biblical word expressing the bond of love, both divine (Deut 10:15) and human, pure (David and Jonathan, 1 Sam 18:1) and impure (Shechem and Dinah, Gen 34:3).

162. Song 1:3, 3:4. The Vulgate has "cellars." Bernard may be following the Old Italic version, which has "chambers," but perhaps it is just a slip for in Div 92:1 he contrasts the "cellar" of Song 1:3 with the "chamber" of Song 3:4 (OB 6-1:346; CF 49).

worthy of this when she learned humility in the school of the Son, listening to his warning: "If you do not know yourself, go forth and pasture your herds."[163] She is twice worthy since she was led by the Holy Spirit from the school of humility to the storehouse of charity,[164] for this is what is meant by guarding the flocks of the neighbors. She was brought there by love, once there she is cushioned by flowers, stayed up with apples,[165] that is by good morals and holy virtues, and finally led into the chamber of the King for whose love she languishes. There for a short time, just one half-hour, while there is silence in heaven,[166] she sleeps in that desired embrace. She sleeps but her heart watches[167] and is fed with the secrets of truth on which later, when she comes to herself, her memory can dwell. There she sees things invisible and hears things unspeakable which it is not given man to utter.[168] They are beyond the knowledge which night can pass on to night for this is the word that day utters to day.[169] Wise men speak wisdom to the wise and spiritual things are made known to the spiritual.[170]

VIII. 22. Paul must have passed through these three degrees when, as he tells us, he was rapt up to the third heaven.[171] Why does he use the word *rapt*, not *led*? It is a lesson for me. If the great Apostle had to be transported to that place which he could not know by his own learning or climb to by his own strength even with a guide, then I, so tiny compared to Paul, must never presume that I can climb to the third heaven by my own strength and effort. I must not presume, but on the other hand I need not be daunted by the difficulty of the journey. He whose way is pointed out to him or who is as-

163. Song 1:7.
164. Song 1:3.
165. Song 2:5. For an alternate and fuller interpretation of this text see Dil 7; OB 3:124f; below, p. 98.
166. Rev 8:1. Concerning the brevity and rarity of this experience see Dil 27; OB 3:142; below, p. 119.
167. Song 5:2.
168. 2 Cor 12:4.
169. Ps 18:3.
170. 1 Cor 2:13.
171. 2 Cor 12:2.

sisted, contributes something by his own efforts to unravel
the problem or go step by step to the goal. He will say: "Not
I, but the grace of God working in me."[172] One who is carried
up, he knows not where, by another's power, contributing
not the slightest effort by his own strength to the action of
his helper, has nothing of which to boast, either in whole or
part. The Apostle could climb to the lowest and the middle
heaven by the help and guidance given him, but to the third
he had to be lifted up. We read that the Son came to help
men to climb to the first heaven,[173] the Holy Spirit was sent[174]
to guide them to the second, but we never read of the Father
that he was sent or came to earth. We must, of course, bear
in mind that he was working with the Son and the Holy Spirit
in all these things. What we do read is: "The earth is filled
with the mercy of the Lord;"[175] "The heavens and the earth
are filled with your glory,"[176] and much more to the same
effect. I read about the Son: "When the fullness of time had
come God sent his Son;"[177] and the Son himself says: "The
Spirit of the Lord has sent me;"[178] and, "And now the Lord
and his Spirit sent me," as we find in the same Prophet.[179]
About the Holy Spirit I read: "The Paraclete, the Holy Spirit
whom the Father will send in my name;"[180] and: "When I
have been lifted up I will send him to you,"[181] speaking of
course about the Holy Spirit. The Father is everywhere in
Person, but I never remember him to have been spoken of
except as being in heaven, as in the Gospel: "My Father who
is in heaven."[182] and in the prayer: "Our Father who art in
heaven."[183]

172. 1 Cor 15:10.
173. Eph 4:9f.
174. Jn 15:26.
175. Ps 32:5.
176. This is found in the acclamation which is sung at the conclusion of the
preface of the canon of the mass. Cf. Is 6:3. Cf. also the sixth verse of the *Te
Deum.*
177. Gal 4:4.
178. Lk 4:18; Is 61:1.
179. Is 48:16.
180. Jn 14:26.
181. Jn 16:7.
182. Mt 16:17.
183. Mt 6:9.

23. My conclusion from all this is that, because the Father did not come down, Paul could not climb up to the third heaven to have sight of him, but he does remember that he was rapt up there.[184] There is, however, another about whom we can speak in a different fashion. "No man has gone up into heaven but the one who came down from heaven."[185] It is not a question here of the first or second heaven for David expressly says to you: "His going forth is from the highest heavens."[186] He was not suddenly snatched up, he was not secretly stolen away, but before the very eyes of the disciples, while they looked on he ascended.[187] Elijah had only one witness.[188] Paul had none since he can hardly be counted witness or judge of the event himself as his own words show: "I know not—God knows."[189] But Christ, having all things in his own power, descended when he willed and ascended when he willed.[190] He decided for himself the place and the time, the day and the hour, and gathered the witnesses he had himself chosen to see this great vision, and in their sight he ascended.[191] Paul was rapt up, Elijah likewise, Enoch was transported.[192] But our Redeemer, as we read, rose by his own power, receiving no help. He was carried by no chariot,[193] assisted by no angel, but through his own power alone, "A cloud received him from their sight."[194] It did not come to help him because he was tired, nor to speed his ascent because he was too slow, not to support him because he was in danger of falling. No! it came to hide him from the carnal eyes of his disciples. Hitherto they knew Christ according to the flesh but they would know him so no more.[195] Those whom the

184. 2 Cor 12:2. Cf. Csi 5:3; OB 468f; CF 19.
185. Jn 3:13.
186. Ps 18:7.
187. Acts 1:9.
188. 2 Kings 2:1.
189. 2 Cor 12:2.
190. Cf. Augustine, *Sermon ad catech.* 8: Christ "was born when he willed and died when he willed."
191. Acts 1:9.
192. Gen 5:24; cf. Heb 11:5.
193. 2 Kings 2:11.
194. Acts 1:9. Cf. Asc 2:6; OB 5:130f; CF 25.
195. 2 Cor 5:16.

Son beckoned to the first heaven by his humiliation, the Spirit brought to the second by charity and the Father raised to the third in contemplation. First they are humiliated in truth and say: "In your truth you have humbled me."[196] Then they rejoice in the truth, singing: "How good and how pleasant it is, brothers dwelling in unity;"[197] for we read that "charity . . . rejoices in truth."[198] Finally, they are carried up to the hidden home of truth itself[199] and there they say: "My secret to myself, my secret to myself! "[200]

IX. 24. What business has a poor wretch like me to do prowling about the two higher heavens, and that not in spirit but only with a flow of empty talk? I have quite work enough for my hands and feet beneath the lowest heaven. Thanks to the help of him who called me I have built a ladder to take me to it. This is my road to God's salvation.[201] Already I see God, resting on the top of the ladder;[202] already I have the joy of hearing the voice of Truth. He calls to me and I reply to him: "Stretch out your right hand to the work of your hands."[203] You have numbered my steps, O Lord,[204] but I am a slow climber, a weary traveller, and I need a resting place. Woe is me if the darkness should overtake me,[205] or if my flight should be in winter or on the Sabbath[206] seeing that now, in an acceptable time, on the day of salvation,[207] I can hardly grope my way to the light. Why am I so slow? O, if any is to me a son, a brother in the Lord, a comrade, one who shares my journey, let him pray for me! Let him pray to the Almighty that he may strengthen the weary foot and not let the foot of pride come nigh to me.[208] The weary foot is a poor help in climbing to the truth, but the other cannot even stand on the place it has gained: "They are cast out, they cannot stand."[209]

196. Ps 118:75.
197. Ps 132:1.
198. 1 Cor 13:6.
199. 2 Cor 12:4.
200. Is 24:16.
201. Ps 49:23.
202. Gen 28:12-13.

203. Job 14:15.
204. Job 14:15.
205. Jn 12:35.
206. Mt 24:20.
207. 2 Cor 6:2.
208. Ps 35:12.
209. Ps 35:13.

25. This is said about any of the proud. What is said about their Head, the "King of all the sons of pride"?[210] "He stood not in the truth;"[211] and "I saw Satan falling from heaven."[212] He fell through nothing but pride. What will be my fate if he perceives haughtiness from afar,[213] sees me to be proud? A terrible voice will sound for me: "You were a son of the Most High but like a man you shall die and like one of the princes fall."[214] Who would not shudder at the thunder of that voice?[215] Jacob was better off when at the stroke of the Angel the sinew of his thigh shrunk[216] than if under the influence of the angel of pride it swelled, collapsed and fell. I wish the Angel would strike my sinew and make it shrink that by this affliction I might begin to advance[217] instead of letting my own strength hurry me on to inevitable ruin. "The weakness of God is stronger than men."[218] The Apostle's sinew was struck by an angel, not of the Lord but of Satan. When he complained the answer was: "My grace is sufficient for you, for virtue[219] is made perfect in infirmity." What virtue? He tells us: "Gladly will I glory in my infirmities that the virtue of Christ may dwell in me."[220] But Christ possesses all virtues; which is he speaking of in particular here? Of all his virtues, and he possessed them all, Christ specially commends one to us, humility. "Learn of me for I am meek and humble of heart."[221]

26. How glad I too should be, Lord Jesus, to glory, if I could, in my infirmity, in the shrinking of my sinew, that your virtue, your humility, might be made perfect in me.

210. Job 41:25.
211. Jn 8:44.
212. Lk 10:18.
213. Ps 137:6.
214. Ps 81:6f.
215. Ps 103:7.
216. Gen 32:25; cf. 2 Cor 12:9; see also SC 29:7; OB 1:208; CF 7.
217. 2 Cor 12:9.
218. 1 Cor 1:25.
219. The *virtus* of the Vulgate should be more properly translated "power" to be true to the thought of St Paul. However, as is evident from the following sentences St Bernard takes it to mean "virtue."
220. 2 Cor 12:7ff.
221. Mt 11:29.

Your grace is sufficient for me when my own virtue fails.
With the foot of grace firmly planted on the ladder of humility, painfully dragging the foot of my own weakness behind
me, I should safely mount upward, until, holding fast to the
truth, I attained the broad plain of charity. There I shall sing
my song of thanksgiving: "You have set my feet on a broad
plain."[222] Thus I warily enter on the narrow way,[223] step by
step safely ascend the steep ladder, and by a kind of miracle
climb to the truth, behind the time perhaps, and limping, but
still with confidence. "Woe is me that my exile is prolonged! [224]
O that I had wings like a dove, that I might fly away" to
truth "and be at rest" in charity! [225] But since I have no
wings, "lead me in your way, O Lord, that I may walk in
your truth"[226] and the truth will make me free.[227] Why did
I ever desert the truth! If I had not been so lightheaded and
stupid as to come down from truth I would not now be faced
with this slow and hard climb back to it. Did I say, "come
down"? "Crash down" would be more like it; though in a
certain sense the milder expression is more suitable because
one does not plunge to the depths of evil in one sudden fall,
no more than one springs to the heights of virtue at one
bound, but has to climb step by step. So the descent too is
spread out little by little,[228] according to the picture given
to us: "The wicked man is proud all the days of his life;"[229]
and, "There are ways that seem to a man right, but their end
leads to evil."[230]

27. You see now there is a way down and a way up, a way
to evil and a way to good. Avoid evil and do good. If you are
not able to do it by your own power—pray! Say with the
Prophet: "Put false ways far from me."[231] How is that to be
done? "Show me the mercy of your law."[232] This law is the
law given to direct those who have wandered from the road,[233]
strayed from the truth. I am among them; I have fallen from

222. Ps 30:9.
223. Mt 7:14.
224. Ps 119:5.
225. Ps 54:7.
226. Ps 85:11.
227. Jn 8:32.

228. Sir 19:1.
229. Job 15:20.
230. Prov 14:12; 16:25.
231. Ps 118:29.
232. *Ibid.*
233. Ps 24:8. See above no. 2, p. 30.

the truth. But "if a man falls will he not rise again?"[234] Yes, and it is in that hope that I have chosen the path of truth,[235] to climb by it, now that I am humbled, to the place from which I fell in my pride. Yes, I will climb back and I will sing: "It is good for me, Lord, that you have humbled me; the law of your mouth is better to me than thousands of silver and gold pieces."[236] David seems to speak of two ways.[237] In fact, there is only one, but there is a distinction and a reason for the two names. The same ladder is for those who come down, the way of iniquity, for those who go up, the way of truth. By the same steps one goes up to the throne and one comes down from it; by the same road one goes to the city and one departs from it; by the same gate one enters and one leaves the house. Indeed, it was by the one same ladder that Jacob saw the angels ascending and descending.[238] What is the bearing of all this? It is that when you wish to return to the truth there is no need to seek an unknown road; it is the same as that by which you came down. On your ascent you will be able to follow the track of the footprints you made in your descent. Now that you are humbled you will climb by the self same steps you trod on as you came down in your pride. The twelfth and lowest step to which your pride brought you is the first step upward of humility and so on in due order: the eleventh is the second; the tenth the third; the ninth the fourth; the eighth the fifth; the seventh the sixth; the sixth the seventh; the fifth the eighth; the fourth the ninth; the third the tenth; the second the eleventh; the first the twelfth. If your conscience has noted these steps of your pride you will recognize them and will have no trouble in finding the way of humility.

234. Jer 8:4; Amos 5:1.
235. Ps 118:30.
236. Ps 118:71f.
237. Ps 1:1,6.
238. Gen 28:12.
239. In classical literature curiosity (*curiositas*) is not taken as a vice. However, the one time it is found in the Vulgate, Num 4:20, it does refer to an inordinate tendency. It is in this biblical sense that Bernard always takes it. See Div 14:2; OB 6-1:135; CF 46; QH 8:5; OB 4:429; CF 43. This would be common among the Fathers also, see e.g., Tertulian, *On Prescription Against Heretics*, 14, tr. C. Dodgson in *Apologetic and Practical Treatises*, 2 ed. (Oxford: Parker, 1854) pp. 463-5.

THE FIRST STEP OF PRIDE: CURIOSITY

X. 28. The first step of pride is curiosity.[239] How does it show itself? You see one who up to this time had every appearance of being an excellent monk. Now you begin to notice that wherever he is, standing, walking or sitting, his eyes are wandering, his glance darts right and left, his ears are cocked. Some change has taken place in him; every movement shows it. "The perverse man winks with his eye, nudges with his foot, points with his finger."[240] These symptoms show his soul has caught some disease. He used to watch over his own conduct; now all his watchfulness is for others. "He does not know himself so he must go forth to pasture his goats."[241] Goats are a symbol of sin and I am applying the word to his eyes and ears. They are the windows through which death creeps into the soul,[242] as death came into the world by sin.[243] These are the flocks the curious man tends, while he lets his soul starve. My man! if you gave yourself the attention you ought, I do not think you would have much time to look after others. Listen, busybody, to Solomon, listen to the words of the Wise Man for a fool: "Guard your heart with all care."[244] Your senses will have quite enough to do to guard the source of life. You wander away from yourself? Whom have you left in charge? Your eyes sweep the heavens.[245] How do you dare, you who have sinned against heaven? Look over the earth, that you might know yourself.[246] It speaks to you of yourself because, "Dust you are and unto dust you shall return."[247]

240. Prov 6:12f.
241. Song 1:7.
242. Jer 9:21. Cf. Conv 10; OB 4:83; CF 43.
243. Rom 5:12.
244. Prov 4:23.
245. In contrast to the publican, Lk 18:13. Bernard places this in contrast to the twelfth step of humility in the *Rule of St Benedict*: ". . . that is to say that whether he is at the work of God, in the oratory, in the monastery, in the garden, on the road, in the fields or anywhere else and whether sitting, walking or standing he should always have his head bowed and his eyes toward the ground . . . " —RB 7:63.
246. *Ut cognascas teipsum*—Bernard might possibly have been familiar with the Delphic Oracle, however, it is probable that he is rather influenced by the passage from the Song of Songs which he so frequently quotes. Cf. SC 36:7; OB 2:8; CF 7.
247. Gen 3:19.

29. Are the eyes never to be raised at all? Yes, but only for two reasons: to look for help, or to help others. David raised his eyes to the mountains to see if help would come to him.[248] Our Lord looked out over the crowd to see if they needed his help.[249] One raised his eyes in misery, the other in mercy—two excellent reasons. If, when time, place and circumstances call for it, you raise your eyes for your own need or your brother's, I certainly will not blame you; I will think all the better of you. Misery is a good excuse; mercy is a very commendable reason. If it is for some motive other than these two that you raise your eyes I am afraid you imitate neither the Prophet nor our Lord but Dinah, Eve, or Satan himself. Dinah was leading her goats to pasture when she was snatched away from her father and despoiled of her virginity.[250] Ah! Dinah! you were anxious to see the foreign woman?[251] What need was there for that? What good did it do you? Was it just idle curiosity? Yes, you were idle, but someone who saw you did not stay idle. You were looking about curiously, but someone eyed you still more curiously. Who would have then believed that your curious idleness or idle curiosity would be fruitful. But it did bear terrible fruit for you and for your family and for your enemies, too.[252]

30. What about you, Eve? You were in Paradise, charged along with your husband to tend it and care for it.[253] If you had kept the command given you, you would have gone in due time to a better place where there is no labor and no care. You were permitted to eat the fruit of every tree except the tree of knowledge of good and evil.[254] The other trees were good and their fruit tasted well.[255] Why did you want the fruit that tasted evil as well? "Be not wiser than it behoves one to be

248. Ps 120:1.
249. Jn 6:5.
250. Song 1:7.
251. Gen 34:1.
252. Gen 34:25ff. Dinah was raped, her brothers acted treacherously, and her lover and all his people were slain or enslaved.
253. Gen 2:15.
254. Gen 2:16.
255. Gen 2:9.

wise."[256] To be wise in evil is not wisdom but foolishness. Keep what is entrusted to you; wait for what is promised to you. Avoid what is forbidden or you will lose what you already have. Why are you so ready to look on death? What do those glances mean? You are forbidden to eat that fruit, why do you look at it? "Oh!" you answer, "I am only looking. I have not so much as put a hand to it. My eyes are under no restriction; I was forbidden only to eat. What did God give me eyes for if I cannot look at whatever I want?" Have you never read; "All things are lawful for me but not all expedient?"[257] The look may not have been a sin itself but there was a sin somewhere in the background. You cannot have been watching very carefully over yourself or you would not have had time for this curiosity. It may not itself be a sin but it is leading you on to sin. You are already guilty of some fault in the matter and more will follow. While your attention was taken up with this the serpent quietly slipped into your heart and his soft words are being spoken, gentle persuasive words, lies to lull fear to sleep. "No, you will not die," he says.[258] He strengthens your attention, he rouses your appetite, he whets your curiosity, he stirs up your greed. While he presents you with a forbidden fruit he steals the gift you have been given. He gave you an apple and stole Paradise. You drink the poison. You will die and be the mother of the dying. Before the first child was born salvation was gone. We are born and we die. We are born dying men, for the doom of death is laid upon us before ever we are born. This is the heavy burden you have laid upon all your sons even to this day.

BERNARD'S OWN OPINION CONCERNING THE APOSTATE SERAPH

31. And you, Satan! made in the likeness of God, placed not in Eden but in the delights of the Paradise of God,[259] what

256. Rom 12:3.
257. 1 Cor 6:12.
258. Gen 3:4.
259. Ezek 28:12. In its literal sense the text has reference to the King of Tyre but the Fathers commonly found in him a type of Satan, e.g., Origen, *Hom. XIII in Ezechielem* 2; PG 13:760.

more did you want? Full of wisdom and perfect in beauty
"seek not what is too high for you, peer not into what is too
mighty."[260] Stay in your own place lest you fall if you walk
in great and wonderful things above you.[261] Why are you
casting those glances towards the North? I see you musing
very earnestly on something. I do not know what it is but it
is something beyond your reach. You say: "I will place my
throne in the North."[262] All else in heaven's courts are standing: you alone presume to sit. You disturb the concord of
your brethren, the peace of the heavenly country, and if it
were possible, even the peace of the Blessed Trinity. Wretch!
to this your curiosity has led you. With reckless insolence you
shock your fellow-citizens and insult your King. "Thousands
of thousands minister to him, ten times a hundred thousand
stand before him."[263] In that court none has a right to sit
save him who sits above the Cherubim,[264] waited on by all.
In an unheard-of way you would distinguish yourself from
others, you pry with insatiable curiosity, push yourself forward
without respect, and would place your throne in heaven and
make yourself the equal of the Most High.[265] What strength are
you depending on? On what course are you embarking? You
fool! Will you think of the measure of your strength and think
of the goal to which you are rushing and how you are going
to get there. Answer plainly: does the Most High know what
you are planning or does he not; and is he willing to let you
do it, or not? His knowledge is unclouded,[265] his will is perfect
in goodness: do you think he can be ignorant of your evil
plots, or that he can approve of them? Or do you think he
knows and opposes them but cannot stop them? I can hardly

260. Sir 3:22.
261. Ps 130:1.
262. Is 14:13 (Old Latin or Italic version). Bernard uses this same version below,
no. 36, p. 64 and also in I Nov 2:5; OB 5:310; CF 34. However he was aware of
the Vulgate version for he used it in QH 11:4; OB 4.451; CF 43.
263. Dan 7:10.
264. Ps 79:2.
265. Is 14:4. Cf. Gregory the Great, *Morals on the Book of Job* 29:18; tr.
J. Newman, Library of the Fathers, vol. 3, part 1 (London: Parker, 1847), p. 314.
266. Job 36:4.
267. Mt 20:15.

believe that even you could doubt the infinite knowledge, power and perfection of your Creator; unless, indeed, you think you needed no Creator. But indeed you did; you came from nothingness and exist entirely by his power. Such as you are he knew you and such as you are he made you. How then can you expect God to consent to what he does not want done and can easily prevent? I wonder have we in you an instance of the common proverb: "Familiarity breeds contempt"? Perhaps indeed it was you who began it, for your like continue. Is your eye evil because he is good?[267] If you draw your confidence from his very goodness, try to remember before whose eyes you flaunt your impudence, before whose might you display your rashness.

32. I expect these are the lines on which your thoughts are running, the evil you plan on your bed:[268] "There is no fear the Creator will destroy the work of his hands. I know that nothing I think is hidden from God, else he would not be God. I know that what I plan does not please him, else he would not be good. I know that if in fact he wills, I cannot escape his hand because he is mighty. But still I have nothing to fear. My designs cannot please him because he is good and I am acting badly. I admit that. But, tell me, would he be willing to act badly himself? I am wrong in going against his will; he would do wrong if he were vindictive. No matter how bad my crime he cannot punish it because he does not wish to lose nor can he lose his quality of goodness." You deceive yourself, you wretch, you deceive yourself, not God.[269] Yes, I repeat you deceive yourself; iniquity deceives itself, not God. You are acting deceitfully, but right before his eyes;[270] and deceiving yourself, not God. You are using his very kindness as an excuse for sinning the more, and thereby making your sin the more hateful.[271] What could be more vile than to turn to the contempt of your Creator the very thing that should make you love him more? Could a worse sin be imagined? You know without any doubt the power of God to destroy you as easily as he created you, and yet trusting in his great kindness

268. Ps 35:5.   270. Ps 35:3.
269. Ps 26:12.   271. *Ibid.*

you hope to escape punishment! This is surely returning evil for good, hatred for love.[272]

33. Your sin deserves, not one swift stroke of punishment, but an eternal reprobation. He is your kindest and most exalted Lord. Yet you want and hope to force yourself on him as an equal, to afflict him constantly with your hateful sight, to have you as an unwanted companion, not destroying you even when he could. He would rather suffer himself than let you perish; he could destroy you if he wished, but, because of his kindness, you think he could not want it. Certainly, if this is what you believe, you are even more evil if you do not love him. If he lets himself suffer rather than have you suffer, how evil it is that you do not spare him who does not spare himself to spare you. But this is nonsense! The divine perfection does not require that kindness hinder justice, as if God could not be both kind and just at the same time.[273] In fact, it is a greater kindness when it is accompanied by justice; kindness too weak to enforce justice would not be a virtue at all. God, in the goodness and freedom of his will made you, and you return no thanks for it; he has spared you the chastisements of his justice and your only return is to cast aside fear and sin more bodly, presuming on continued impunity.

You pay lip-service to the goodness of God; you have yet to feel his justice. You will be entangled in the very coils you placed to trip your Maker. Your cleverness argues that while you planned harm for him and he could avoid it if he wished, you think he will not so wish, for fear he should lose goodness, which you allow him only because you have never seen him inflicting punishment. The grief will come back on your own head. God is infinitely just and so he cannot, must not, allow an offence against his goodness to go unpunished. Still, his goodness tempers your doom. He will not refuse pardon if you are willing to repent. But the hardness of your impenitent heart will not let you repent.[274] You must suffer.

34. Where has Satan gone wrong? God says: "Heaven is my throne, earth my footstool."[275] He does not say "the"

272. Ps 108:5.
273. Ps 24:8.

274. Rom 2:5. Cf. Gra 29; CF 19.
275. Is 66:1; Acts 7:49.

east or "the" west or any other particular region of heaven, but "the whole heaven is my footstool." Therefore, Satan, you cannot enthrone yourself in the heavens[276] for God claims all. Neither have you a place on earth; for that is his footstool.[277] Indeed it is on the firm earth where the Church sits, founded on solid rock.[278] What will you do? You are thrown out of heaven and there is no place for you on earth. Only the air remains for you, to hover there, not to sit.[279] You tried to unsettle the stability of eternity and your doom is an eternal restlessness. You must be tossed about between heaven and earth while the Lord sits on his high and exalted throne and the whole earth is filled with his glory;[280] and you have no place except the air.

35. Some of the Seraphim use the wings of their contemplation to fly from the throne to the footstool, from the footstool back to the throne; others veil with their wings the face and feet of the Lord.[281] We can learn from this, I think,[282] that, as the Cherubim were posted at the gate of Paradise to bar it to sinful man,[283] so the Seraphim check your impudent and imprudent curiosity that you might not be allowed to pierce the mysteries either of heaven or of the Church on earth. You must be content with the hearts of the proud, who will not stoop to live like the rest of men on earth and may not soar to heaven like the angels. Although the Head who is in heaven and the "feet" on earth are hidden from you, nevertheless you are allowed to see something of what is in between so that you might be envious. While suspended in air you will see the angels descending and ascending[284] as they pass you in their flight, but what they hear in heaven and what they announce on earth are hidden from you.

276. Rev 12:8.
277. Mt 5:35.
278. Mt 7:25.
279. Eph 2:2.
280. Is 6:1ff.
281. Is 6:2.
282. See above, Retractation, p. 25.
283. Gen 3:24. Bernard describes the role of each of the ranks of the angels in Csi 5:8 (OB 3:472f; CF 19) and more fully in SC 19:2-6 (OB 1:109-12; CF 4:141-4).
284. Gen 28:12.

36. Lucifer, you who rise in the morning[285]—no, not Lucifer
the Lightbearer, but Nightbearer and Deathbearer—your true
course was from East to South, why did you swerve to the
North? The higher you would climb the swifter your fall.
Nevertheless I am curious, O Envious One, to know more
about the course of your curiosity.[286] You say: "I will place
my throne in the North."[287] I know of course that you are
a spirit and there is no question here of the North Pole of this
earth. The North stands for the reprobate and your throne is
your kingdom over them. Now, you were once very close to
God and in his foreknowledge[288] you might have seen the
future more clearly than could others. You foresaw these
reprobate men shining with no ray of wisdom, burning with
no flame of love and of this empty wasteland you chose to be
lord, to infuse into them the light of your own cunning, to
inflame them with your own evil desires. The Most High God
rules over the children of obedience[289] in his love and goodness;
and you would be king of the sons of pride[290] in your clever
malice and your malicious cleverness and so be like the Most
High.[291] But tell me, for it is this which makes me wonder: if
in the foreknowledge of God you saw your lordship, did you
not also foresee your downfall? And if you did foresee it,
what madness made you choose such wretched dignity, pre-
fering to rule in misery rather than be subject in happiness?
Would it not have been better to share with the sons of light
than to be the leader of the sons of darkness?[292] I find it
easier to believe that you did not foresee it. Or perhaps, as I
suggested already, you looked to the goodness of God and

285. Is 14:12. Cf. with the passage in I Nov 5:7-8. According to its literal sense
the text of Is does not refer to Satan but rather to the King of Babylon. However
the Fathers commonly see here a type of the evil angel, finding some basis in
Lk 10:18.
286. Typical Bernardine alliteration: *Velim tamen curiosius, curiose, intentionem
tuae curiositatis inquirere.*
287. See above, note 262.
288. 1 Pet 1:2.
289. 1 Pet 1:14.
290. Job 41:25.
291. Is 14:14.
292. Eph 6:12.

said to yourself: "He will not take notice."[293] Or it may be that the vision of your coveted princedom was a beam of pride[294] blinding your eye so that it could not see the fall.

37. It is quite possible that one could really foresee the future in a spirit of prophecy and yet be ignorant of some details. These gaps in his knowledge need not make us conclude that the whole prophecy was a delusion. We have a case of this in Joseph. He foresaw his own future greatness[295] but did not foresee his sale as a slave,[296] though that came before his triumph. I do not think the great Patriarch was guilty of pride. I am only using him as an example. Still, if anyone would hold that he was guilty of vanity when he spoke about his dreams in his young days when their mystery was still unknown I would think it was less vanity than the greatness of the mystery, or a boy's simplicity. However, if he was guilty of any vanity he was able to make up for it by all he suffered. Some have pleasant things foretold to them at times and it would not be human if there was not some touch of vanity either at the fact of the revelation or at the things promised.[297] That would not prevent the prophecy from being fulfilled though there could be some punishment for the vanity. Our heavenly Physician does not always treat our moral sores with ointment. They may be too infected for that. He will at need cauterize or lance them, sending temptations and afflictions to the chosen soul to crush and humiliate it so that its joy is turned into sorrow[298] and its revelation now seems a delusion. It is preserved from vanity; but the revelation still stands true. St Paul's pride was kept down by a sting of the flesh but he was lifted up by his many revelations.[299] Zachary was punished by dumbness for his unbelief[300] but the angel's prophecy did not fail.[301] The saints always go forward, in honor or dishonor.[302] If they are ever led to think too much of themselves by their gifts and fall into the human weakness of vanity, they will very quickly be reminded of what they really are.

293. Ps 9:34.
294. Mt 7:3.
295. Gen 37:5-10.
296. Gen 37:28.
297. Cf 2 Cor 12:7.

298. Bar 4:34; Jas 4:9.
299. 2 Cor 12:7.
300. Lk 1:20.
301. Lk 1:57ff.
302. 2 Cor 6:8.

38. How did we get on to this matter of revelations while we were talking of curiosity? I wandered off into this by-path when I was trying to show that the reprobate angel could have foreseen the dominion he was later to have over fallen men and still not foresee his own damnation. In the meantime we have opened up a good many minor questions and have not answered them. However, the sum total is: he fell from truth by curiosity[303] when he turned his attention to something he coveted unlawfully and had the presumption to believe he could gain. Curiosity was the beginning of all sin[304] and so is rightly considered the first step of pride. Unless it is checked promptly it leads to the second step: levity.

THE SECOND STEP: LEVITY OF MIND

XI. 39. The monk who observes others instead of attending to himself will begin before long to see some as his superiors and others as his inferiors; in some he will see things to envy, in others, things to despise. The eyes have wandered and the mind soon follows. It is no longer steadily fixed on its real concerns and is now carried up on the crest of the waves of pride, now down in the trough of envy. One minute the man is full of envious sadness, the next childishly glad about some excellence he sees in himself. The former is evil, the latter, vain; both bespeak pride because it is love of one's own excellence[305] that makes one weep when he is surpassed and rejoice in surpassing others. His conversation will show how his mind is tossed up and down. One moment he is sulky and silent except for some bitter remarks; the next sees a full spate of silly chatter. Now he is laughing, now doleful; all without rhyme or reason.

If now you care to compare these two steps of pride with the last two of humility you will find that they correspond;

303. Cf. Div 14:2; OB 6-1:135; CF 46.
304. Sir 10:15.
305. See above, note 106, p. 42.

curiosity with the last[306] and levity with the second last;[307] and the same will hold for all others, if they are compared one with the other. We will proceed now to the third step of pride—to teach it, not I hope, to practise it.

THE THIRD STEP: GIDDINESS[308]

XII. 40. The proud always seek what is pleasant and try to avoid what is troublesome. In the words of Scripture: "Where there is gladness, there is the heart of the fool."[309] The monk that has come down the two steps of curiosity and levity of mind will find much to upset him. He is saddened every time he sees the goodness of others, impatient with humiliation. He finds an escape in false consolations. His eyes are closed to anything that shows his own vileness or the excellence of others, wide open to what flatters himself. He is largely saved now from his moody exaltation and depression; he has retired into a happy cloud-land. This is the third step. There are indications by which you can know when you yourself or another have reached this point. Watch such a man and you will never notice anything like a tear or a sigh. His appearance is that of

306. "The twelfth degree of humility is that a monk not only have humility in his heart but also by his very appearance make it always manifest to those who see him. That is to say that whether he is at the Work of God, in the oratory, in the monastery, in the garden, on the road, in the fields or anywhere else, and whether sitting, walking or standing, he should always have his head bowed and his eyes toward the ground. Feeling the guilt of his sins at every moment, he should consider himself already present at the dread Judgment and constantly say in his heart what the publican in the Gospel said with his eyes fixed on the earth: "Lord, I am a sinner and not worthy to lift up my eyes to heaven." and again with the Prophet: "I am bowed down and humbled everywhere."—RB 7:62-66.

307. "The eleventh degree of humility is that when a monk speaks he do so gently and without laughter, humbly and seriously, in few and sensible words, and that he be not noisy in his speech. It is written, 'A wise man is known by the fewness of his words.' "—RB 7:60-61. Bernard's descriptive *semper vero irrationabilia . . . verba* is in contrast to Benedict's *pauca verba et rationabilia.*

308. In Gra 14 Bernard brings out how truly miserable is this giddiness or false joy: *Nulla autem verior miseria, quam falsa laetitia.* (OB 3:176; CF 19). More important he points out the source of true joy: hope in the Lord rather than in self—SC 37:3; OB 2:10; CF 7.

309. Eccles 7:5.

a man who is forgetful of what he is or at least is now purified of all trace of sin. He is scurrilous[310] in sign-making,[311] over-cheerful in appearance, swaggering in his bearing, always ready for a joke, any little thing quickly gets a laugh.[312] He is careful not to remember anything he has done which could hurt his self-esteem; but all his good points will be remembered, and added up, and if need be, touched up by imagination. He thinks only of what he wants and never of what is permitted. At times he simply cannot stop laughing or hide his empty-headed merriment. He is like a well-filled bladder that has been pricked and squeezed. The air, not finding a free vent, whistles out through the little hole with squeak after squeak. The rule of silence[313] will not let a monk relieve himself of his vain thoughts and silly jokes. They gather pressure inside until they burst out in giggles.[314] In embarrassment he buries his face in his hands, tightens his lips, clenches his teeth. It is no use! The laughter must explode and if his hand holds it in his mouth, it bursts out through his nose.

THE FOURTH STEP: BOASTING

XIII. 41. When vanity has swelled the bladder to its limits a bigger vent must be made or the bladder will burst. As the monk's silly merriment grows, laughing and signs are not

310. Scurrility is quite strongly reprobated by the Benedictine Rule: "But as for scurrility and idle words or words that move to laughter, these we condemn everywhere with a perpetual ban, and for such conversation we do not permit a disciple to open his mouth."—RB 6:8.

311. Not only the Cistercians but many of the Black Monks of this time shared a common sign language whose origins are lost in abscurity. It is still employed in some monasteries. See R. Barakat, *The Cistercian Sign Language: A Study in Non-verbal Communication,* Cistercian Studies Series 11 (Spencer, Mass.: Cistercian Publications, 1972).

312. *Facilius ac promptus in risu*—RB 7:59, where Benedict uses it to describe the tenth step of humility by negation.

313. This is found especially in RB 6, the chapter immediately preceeding the steps of humility. For a thorough study of the provisions in RB for silence see Ambrose Wathen, OSB, *Silence: The Meaning of Silence in the Rule of St Benedict,* Cistercian Studies Series 22 (Spencer, Mass.: Cistercian Publications, 1972).

314. Bernard might have had in mind here Persius, *Satires* 3:8: *ingeminant tremulos naso crispante cachinnos,* especially in view of his use of *cachinnos* on the way he ends the paragraph. See *The Satires of A. Persius Flaccus,* tr. J. Covington, ed. H. Nettleship, 3 ed. (Oxford: Clarendon, 1893), pp. 66-7.

enough outlet, and he says like Elihu: "Behold, my heart is
like new wine that has no vent; like new wineskins it is ready
to burst."[315] Yes, speak or burst! He is full of words and the
swelling spirit strains within him.[316] His hunger and thirst are
for listeners, someone to listen to his boasting, on whom he
can pour out all his thoughts, someone he can show what a
big man he is. At last the chance to speak comes. The discussion turns on literature. He brings forth from his treasury
old things and new.[317] He is not shy about producing his
opinions; words are bubbling over. He does not wait to be
asked. His information comes before any question. He asks
the questions; gives the answers; cuts off anyone who tries
to speak.[318] When the bell rings and it is necessary to interrupt the conversation, hour-long though it be, he seeks a minute more. He must get special permission to resume his talk,
not to edify the listeners, but to show off his learning.[319] He
may have the capacity to help others but that is the least of
his concerns. His aim is not to teach you nor to be taught by
you, but to show how much he knows. If the conversation
brings up the subject of religion, he is quite ready to talk of
visions and dreams. He warmly recommends fasting, urges
watching and exalts prayer above all. He will give a long dis-
course on patience and humility and each of the other virtues—
all words, all bragging. He trusts that you will draw the conclusion: "Out of the abundance of the heart the mouth
speaks;"[320] or, "A good man from a good treasure brings
forth good things."[321] The talk takes a lighter turn. He is
more in his element here and becomes really eloquent. If
you hear him, you will say his mouth has become a fountain
of wit, a river of smart talk. He can set the most grave and

315. Job 32:19.
316. Job 32:18.
317. Mt 13:52.
318. Mills has this note: Contrast St Basil's standard for the true monk (Ep 11,
tr. Newman, *Church of the Fathers,* Basil and Gregory, 5): "To interrogate without overearnestness; to answer without desire of display; not to interrupt a prof-
itable speaker, nor to desire ambitiously to put in a word of one's own."
319. Cf. 1 Cor 8:1.
320. Mt 12:34.
321. Mt 12:35.

serious laughing heartily.[322] To say it briefly, when words
are many, boasting is not lacking.[323] There is the fourth step
described and identified. Flee the reality, but remember the
name. The same warning goes with the next, which I name
singularity.

THE FIFTH STEP: SINGULARITY

XIV. 42. When a man has been bragging that he is better
than others he would feel ashamed of himself if he did not
live up to his boast and show how much better than others
he is. The common rule of the monastery and the example of
the seniors are no longer enough for him.[324] He does not so
much want to be better as to be seen to be better. He is not
so much concerned about leading a better life as appearing
to others to do so. He can then say "I am not like the rest of
men."[325] He is more complacent about fasting for one day
when the others are feasting than about fasting seven days
with all the rest. He prefers some petty private devotion to
the whole night office of psalms.[326] While he is at his meals
he casts his eyes around the tables and if he sees anyone eating
less than himself he is mortified at being outdone and promptly
and cruelly deprives himself of even necessary food. He would
rather starve his body than his pride. If he sees anyone more
thin, anyone more pallid, he despises himself. He is never at
rest. He wonders what others think about the appearance of
his face and as he cannot see it[327] he must only guess whether

322. Cf. Csi 2:22; OB 3:430; CF 19.

323. Cf. Prov 10:19; RB 7:56-58: "The ninth degree of humility is that a monk
restrain his tongue and keep silence, not speaking until he is questioned. For the
Scripture shows that "in much speaking there is no escape from sin" and that "the
talkative man is not stable on the earth."

324. RB 7:55: "The eighth degree of humility is that a monk do nothing except
what is commended by the common Rule of the monastery and the example of the
elders." Cf. SC 19:7, OB 1:112f, CF 4:145; SC 64:5; 2:168, CF 31.

325. Lk 18:11.

326. According to the RB, which the Cistercians strictly followed, fourteen
psalms were recited or sung at the night office early in the morning: RB 9.
Guerric of Igny, a close disciple of Bernard, who follows him in many things,
emphasizes this same point in his Fifth Advent Sermon, 5:2; CF 8:32-33.

327. Needless to say there were no mirrors in the early Cistercian monasteries,
indeed they were only commonly introduced in the middle of this century when
the monks began to shave themselves.

it is rosy or wan by looking at his hands and arms, poking at his ribs, and feeling his shoulders and loins to see how skinny or fleshy they are. He is very exact about his own particular doings and slack about the common exercises. He will stay awake in bed and sleep in choir. After sleeping through the night office while the others were singing psalms, he stays to pray alone in the oratory while they are resting in the cloister.[328] He makes sure that those sitting outside know he is there modestly hidden in his corner, clearing his throat and coughing and groaning and sighing.[329] Some of the more simple-minded are misled by his worthless singularities and, judging by his actions which they see and not seeing the hidden intentions, they canonize the unfortunate man and confirm him in his self-delusion.

THE SIXTH STEP: SELF-CONCEIT

XV. 43. He swallows all the praise others give him. He is quite complacent about his conduct and he never examines his motives now; the good opinion of others is all he needs. About everything else he thinks he knows more than anybody, but when they say something favorable about him he believes them against his own conscience. So now not only in words and affected conduct does he display his piety but he believes in his inmost heart that he is holier than others.[330] It never occurs to him that the praise given to him comes from

328. RB 8:3. Cf. Gilbert of Swineshead, SC 23:3, PL 184-120, CF 14.

329. This is the exact opposite of what St Benedict prescribes: "When the Work of God is ended, let all go out in perfect silence and let reverence for God be observed, so that any brother who may wish to pray privately will not be hindered by another's misconduct. At other times also, if anyone should want to pray by himself, let him go in simply and pray, not in a loud voice but with tears and fervor of heart. He who does not say his prayers this way, therefore, shall not be permitted to remain in the oratory when the Work of God is ended, lest another be hindered, as we have said."—RB 52:2-5.

330. Bernard uses Benedict's own expression to bring out the contrast: "The seventh degree of humility is that he consider himself lower and of less account than anyone else, and this not only in verbal protestation but also *with the most heartfelt inner conviction*, humbling himself and saying with the Prophet, 'But I am a worm and no man, the scorn of men and the outcast of the people. After being exalted, I have been humbled and covered with confusion.' And again, 'It is good for me that you have humbled me, that I may learn your commandments.' " —RB 7:51-54. [Italics mine].

ignorance or kindness; his pride thinks it only his due. So, after singularity, self-conceit comes sixth, and the seventh is presumption.

THE SEVENTH STEP: PRESUMPTION[331]

XVI. 44. When a man thinks he is better than others will he not put himself before others? He must have the first place in gatherings, be the first to speak in council. He comes without being called. He interferes without being asked. He must rearrange everything, re-do whatever has been done. What he himself did not do or arrange is not rightly done or properly arranged. He is the judge of all judges and decides every case beforehand. If he is not made Prior[332] when a vacancy occurs he knows that the Abbot is jealous of him, or has been deceived! If obedience calls him to some ordinary tasks he refuses disdainfully.[333] A man fitted for higher positions could not be occupied with lesser things. Since he is so liberal, even reckless, in offering his services, sooner or later he will make some blunders. Then a superior may have to correct him. Will he admit his fault? He could hardly believe that he could be wrong and certainly will not let anybody else believe it. Thus his fault is made worse instead of being set right. If therefore, when he is corrected, you see him making excuses in his sin[334] you will know he has dropped another step—the eighth, which is named self-justification.

331. Cf. with the treatment of presumption in QH 11:4; OB 4:451; CF 43.

332. Benedict provides in RB 65 that the abbot might choose a *praepositus,* a claustral prior, as a second in command. This was the common practice in Cistercian monasteries.

333. This is just the opposite of the sixth step of humility: "The sixth step of humility is that a monk be content with the poorest and worst of everything, and that in every occupation assigned he consider himself a bad and worthless workman, saying with the Prophet, "I am brought to nothing and I am without understanding; I have become as a beast of burden before you, and I am always with you."—RB 7:49-50.

334. Ps 140:4. Bernard uses this verse as it is found in the Vulgate as his bridge between this and the following step: "Incline not my heart to evil words; to make excuses in sins."

EIGHTH STEP: SELF-JUSTIFICATION

XVII.   45. There are many ways of excusing sins.[335] One will say: "I didn't do it." Another; "I did it, but I was perfectly right in doing it." If it was wrong he may say: "It isn't all that bad." If it was decidedly harmful, he can fall back on: "I meant well." If the bad intention is too evident he will take refuge in the excuses of Adam and Eve and say someone else led him into it.[336] If a man defends his obvious sins like that, he is hardly likely to fulfill the fifth degree of humility in St Benedict's Rule and "make known to his Abbot by humble confession the evil thoughts of his heart and the sins he has committed in secret."[337]

THE NINTH STEP: HYPOCRITICAL CONFESSION

XVIII.   46. Excuses of this kind are bad enough for the Psalmist to call them "words of malice," but there is something even more dangerous than this stubborn and obstinate self-defence, and that is hypocritical confession springing from pride.[338] There are some who, when they are caught out in wrong-doing and know that if they defend themselves they will not be believed, find a subtle way out of the difficulty in deceitful self-accusation. This is the kind of man "who humbles himself deceitfully while his mind is full of evil."[339] Their

335. See previous note.

336. Gen 3:12-13. See Pre 27 where Bernard, citing the same Ps text (140:4) develops his comment on Adam and Eve, finding the greater sin in this excuse-making (OB 3:272f; CF 1:126).

337. RB 7:44. The early *Consuetudines* of the Cistercians following RB 46, provided for two kinds of confession: open public confession in chapter and private secret confession to the prior at the end of chapter or at other suitable times. See *Consuetudines Ordinis Cisterciensis* III, c. 70 in *Nomasticon Cisterciense*, ed H. Séjalon (Solesmes: St Peter's, 1892), pp. 145ff; also *Usus Conversorum* 11, *ibid.*, p. 239.

338. Bernard speaks of the properties of confession in Div 40:6, the first of which is that it be "true." It is also to be complete and personal, not involving others—*vera, nuda et propria* (OB 6-1:239f; CF 46). The seven steps in the ways of obedience and confession developed by St Bernard in that Sermon might be fruitfully compared with these steps of humility.

339. Sir 19:23.

eyes are cast down, they humble themselves to the very dust, they wring out some tears if they can, sighs and groans interrupt their words. They will not merely admit what has happened but will exaggerate their guilt. They accuse themselves of things so great, so incredible, that you begin to doubt the charges you were certain of before. The things they say about themselves now can surely not be true, perhaps the other things are not so certain either. They are making statements they do not want you to believe, they defend the fault by confessing and hide it by false openness. The confession sounds very well but evil is hidden in the heart. The hearer is led to think that the accusation is not really true, it is only humility. After all, the Scripture says: "The just man is his own first accuser."[340] Such men are willing that you think they are telling lies about themselves, so long as you do not think they are failing in humility. They will not get much credit from God for either truth or humility. If their guilt is too great for any defence they will assume the attitude of penitents hoping that their fault will be forgotten in admiration of their candid confession; but the candor of their confession is all in outward show. It does not come from the heart and cancels no sin.

47. Pride is certainly paying a compliment to humility if it uses it as a disguise when it would escape punishment. The superior will see through this fraud quickly enough if instead of taking notice of this proud humiliation he refuses to overlook the offense or remit the punishment. An earthen vessel is tested by fire[341] and the true penitent by tribulation. A real penitent is not afraid of the difficulties of penance.[342] Whatever is enjoined upon him for the fault which he hates, he patiently embraces with a quiet mind. If obedience should expose him to hard and mortifying things and even undeserved reproaches he will bear it unflinchingly. He has possession of the fourth degree of humility.[343] The man whose penitence

---

340. Prov 18:17 (Old Latin or Italic version).

341. Sir 27:6.

342. Cf. Conv 6; OB 4:77f; CF 43.

343. "The fourth degree of humility is that he hold fast to patience with a silent mind when in this obedience he meets with difficulties and contradictions and even any kind of injustice, enduring all without growing weary or running away." —RB 7:35-36.

is fraudulent will show soon enough that it was a sham humility if he is given the slightest reproach or penance. He murmurs and growls and gets vexed. No, he is not in the fourth degree of humility but the ninth of pride which we have called hypocritical confession. You can judge for yourself what is now the state of this proud man's mind. His fraud has failed him, his peace of mind is gone, his reputation has been lowered, and his sin is unforgiven. Now everybody knows what he is,[344] everyone condemns him, and they are all the more vexed because of the good opinion his fraud fooled them into holding for so long. In the end the superior will find himself forced to be unsparing so as to avoid general scandal.

THE TENTH STEP: REVOLT

XIX. 48. The divine mercy may yet rescue such a man and inspire him to submit to the judgment of the community;[345] but such a character finds this a very hard thing to do, and instead, he may take an attitude of brazen insolence and in desperation take the fatal plunge as far as the tenth step of pride. He has already shown his contempt for his brethren by insolence, and now his contempt for superiors flashes out in open revolt.

49. We may pause here to take notice that I have divided the descent of pride into twelve steps and these again may be grouped into three classes; in the first six contempt is

344. It would seem from this that Bernard, in this step, has in mind the public confession made in chapter. See note 337 above.

345. Bernard has undoubtedly in mind here RB 28: "If a brother who has been frequently corrected for some fault, and even excommunicated, does not amend, let a harsher correction be applied, that is, let the punishment of the rod be administered to him. But if he still does not reform or perhaps (which God forbid) even rises up in pride and wants to defend his conduct, then let the abbot do what a wise physician would do. Having used applications, the ointments of exhortation, the medicines of the Holy Scriptures, finally the cautery of excommunication and of the strokes of the rod, if he sees that his efforts are of no avail, let him apply a still greater remedy, his own prayers and those of all the brethren, that the Lord, who can do all things, may restore health to the sick brother. But if he is not healed even in this way, then let the abbot use the knife of amputation, according to the Apostle's words, 'Expel the evil one from your midst,' and again, 'If the faithless one departs, let him depart,' lest one diseased sheep contaminate the whole flock."

shown for the brethren, in the next four for the superior, in the last two, on which I have not yet touched, contempt for God. We may note too, that the first two steps of humility will have been climbed before entering the community, and, correspondingly, the last two steps of pride will not be reached while one still remains a member. The reason why the first two steps of humility must be climbed before entering is found in the Rule which says: "The third step is that a monk submit himself to a superior in all obedience for the love of God."[346] This submission to a superior takes place when the novice enters the monastery, so he must already have climbed the first two steps. But if a monk refuses to live in harmony with his brethren or to obey his superior, what is he doing in the monastery except causing scandal?

THE ELEVENTH STEP: FREEDOM TO SIN

XX. 50. The man in revolt has reached the tenth step of pride and will leave or be expelled from the monastery. Without delay he goes down to the eleventh step. He then sets his feet on ways that seem to a man right[347] but which will lead him, if God does not block his way,[348] to the depths of hell, to contempt of God. "When wicked man reaches the depths of evil, he is full of contempt."[349] We may style this eleventh step freedom in sinning. The monk has no longer a superior to fear nor brethren to respect, so with fewer qualms he happily gives himself up to his sinful desires which in the monastery fear and shame held in check. He has no abbot or fellow-religious to fear now, but he still keeps some scant fear of God. His conscience still gives some murmurs, however faint; he makes a few half-hearted resolutions, still hesitates a little in his first steps in evil. He does not plunge headlong into the torrent of vice but feels his way step by step like one trying a ford.

346. RB 7:34.
347. Prov 14:12, 16:25. See above, no. 19, p. 46.
348. Cf. Hos 2:6.
349. Prov 18:3 (Old Latin or Italic). Cf. Conv 23; OB 4:95; CF 43; Pre 40; OB 3:280; CF 1:135.

THE TWELFTH STEP: THE HABIT OF SINNING

XXI. 51. The first steps in sin are taken apprehensively and no blow falls from the dreaded judgment of God.[350] Pleasure in sin has been experienced. Sin is repeated and the pleasure grows. Old desires revive, conscience is dulled,[351] habit tightens its grasp. The unfortunate man sinks into the evil depths,[352] is tangled in his vices and is swept into the whirlpool of sinful longings while his reason and the fear of God are forgotten and "the fool says in his heart: There is no God."[353] Good or evil means nothing to him now.[354] He is ready to serve sin heart, hand, and foot with thoughts, acts, and plans unchecked. He seeks new ways of sinning. The plans of his heart, the ready words of his mouth, the works of his hands, are at the service of every impulse. He has become malevolent, evil-speaking, vile.

The just man who has climbed all the steps of humility runs on to life with a ready heart and with the ease of good habit;[355] the evil man who has dropped down to the bottom is ruled by evil habit, and unchecked by fear he runs boldly on to death. Those in mid-course, whether going up or down, are weary with the strain, torn now by the fear of hell and now by the attraction of old habits. Only at the top and at the bottom is there a free and effortless course, upward to life or downward to death; bounding on in the effortless energy of love, or hurried, unresisting, by the downward pull of cupidity. In one case love, in the other apathy ignores the

---

350. Heb 10:27.
351. Cf. Conv 5; OB 4:76; CF 43.
352. Prov 18:3.
353. Ps 13:1.
354. Cf. Pre 39; OB 3:280; CF 1:134.
355. Cf. RB 7:67ff: "Having climbed all these steps of humility, therefore, the monk will presently come to that perfect love of God which casts out fear. And all those precepts which formerly he had not observed without fear, he will now begin to keep by reason of that love, without any effort, as though naturally and by habit. No longer will his motive be the fear of hell, but rather the love of Christ, good habit and delight in the virtues which the Lord will deign to show forth by the Holy Spirit in his servant now cleansed from vice and sin." See also, RB Prol 49.

labor of life. Perfect love or complete malice cast out fear.[356] Security is found in truth or in blindness. So we can call the twelfth step the habit of sinning, by which the fear of God has been lost, replaced by contempt.

XXII. 52. "For such a one," says St John the Apostle, "I would not that anyone should pray."[357] What then, O Blessed Apostle, is he to despair? One who really loves him will still weep. Let him not dare to pray, nor cease to wail. I am not suggesting that hope is entirely gone when prayer is forbidden. I can give you an example of one who believed and hoped even when the case seemed to be beyond prayer. "Lord," she said, "If you had been here my brother would not have died."[358] She must have had faith, strong faith, if she believed that our Lord's presence could have saved her brother's life. Her next words leave us no room for thinking that there was a limit to her faith or that she thought that while our Lord could have saved her brother's life he could not raise him from the dead. She added: "But even now I know that whatever you ask from God he will give to you."[359] When Jesus asked where they had laid him she answered: "Come and see."[360] Why did she stop at that? Martha, you have given us a wonderful example of faith, surely you do not begin to doubt now? When you said: "Come and see," was your hope not strong enough to add: "and raise him up?" If you had no hope you would not have troubled the Master with a useless visit. It is rather that faith will sometimes gain what prayer hardly dares ask. As he approached the grave you stopped him and said: "Lord, by this time there will be an odor for he has been now four days dead."[361] Was it despair made you say that? I rather think you

356. 1 Jn 4:18; RB 7:67.
357. 1 Jn 5:16. See Augustine of Hippo, *City of God* 21:24, tr. G. Walsh and D. Honan, *Works of St Augustine* 8, Fathers of the Church 24 (New York: Fathers of the Church, 1954) pp. 387ff.
358. Jn 11:21. The reference is to Martha speaking of Lazarus' death.
359. Jn 11:22.
360. Jn 11:34. These words however are attributed in the text to the crowd.
361. Jn 11:39.

were making a timid suggestion; just as our Lord after his resurrection feigned to be going further when he really wanted to remain with his disciples.[362] O you two holy sisters,[363] friends of Christ, if you really love your brother why do you not ask for him the mercy of One whose power you cannot doubt, about whose love you can have no hesitation?[364] But their answer comes: "We are praying, praying all the better when we voice no prayer. We trust all the more strongly when we seem to doubt. We show our faith, we show our love; and he who needs no telling knows what we desire.[365] We know that he can do all things; even this great unheard-of miracle is well within his power; but it is far beyond all the merits of our lowliness. It is enough for us to have brought him, to have set the stage for this great wonder, to have given love its opportunity. We would rather wait patiently on his will than ask impudently for something he may not will to give. Perhaps our modesty will supply for our unworthiness." I think of the case of Peter, too, weeping after his great fall, with no express words of prayer, and leaving me no doubt about his pardon.[366]

53. Learn from the Mother of our Lord herself a lesson of how great faith in his wonderful powers can be expressed with modesty. She shows us how modesty, avoiding all presumption, is an ornament to faith. "They have no wine," she said.[367] How briefly and modestly she suggested a request her kindness had so much at heart! And thus you learn that in such circumstances it is better to make a gentle complaint than to insist on a right, better to give modest and gentle expression to the impetuosity of kindly anxiety than to speak in the tone of one who takes it for granted that the request must be heard. She did not speak out unhesitatingly and boldly before everyone: "Listen, Son, they have no wine. The guests are disappointed, the bridegroom is upset; show what you can do." This would not have been too strong an expres-

362. Lk 24:28.
363. Martha and her sister, Mary. Jn 11:1.
364. Jn 11:3: "Lord, he whom you love is sick."
365. Wis 7:27, Mt 6:8.
366. Mt 26:75; Mk 14:72; Lk 22:61-62.
367. Jn 2:3.

sion, certainly, for her affection for those concerned. But this loving mother went privately to her Son, not testing his power but enquiring about what he wished to do. "They have no wine," she said. Could it be expressed more modestly and more trustfully? Her love was sure, her words earnest, her desires prevailing.[368] If then his mother would not presume on her motherhood to ask in so many words for the miracle of the wine, could a lowly slave like myself, honored enough by being the slave of Mother and Son, dare to ask for such a thing as the life of one four days dead?

54. We read in the Gospel of two blind men who were cured. One had lost his sight,[369] and other was born blind.[370] To one sight was restored, to the other given for the first time. The one who lost his sight pleaded pitifully and merited marvelous mercy; but the mercy shown to the other appears more marvelous for he had never asked before receiving the gift of light from his Lord. Finally the former heard the words: "Your faith has made you whole;" but not the latter. We read of two recently deceased[371] and one four days dead being raised to life.[372] For one only, while she still lay in the house, was a plea made by her father, to the others it was the unasked-for gift of love.

55. So, if a similar case should arise—which God forbid—that one of our brethren should die the death, not of the body but of the soul, I, sinner though I be, would plead for him[373] with my Savior with my own most earnest prayers and with the prayers of the brethren. If he returns to life[374] we will have gained our brother.[375] If we should not merit to be heard and he is borne out from among us—because, being dead, he cannot bear the company of the living, or because they cannot

368. Cf. O Asspt 10; OB 5:270; CF 26.
369. Mk 10:46-52; Lk 18:35-43.
370. Jn 9.
371. Jairus' daughter (Mt 9: 18-26; Mk 5: 22-43; LK 8:41-56) and the son of the widow of Naim (Lk 7:11-17).
372. Jn 11:1-44.
373. Bernard has "*pulsabo . . . Salvatorem,* literally "knock on my Savior," suggested by Mt 7:7.
374. Cf. Lk 15:24.
375. Mt 18:15.

bear his company—I will still do my duty as a mourner though I cannot now pray with the same confidence. I do not dare to say: "Lord come, and raise up our dead brother," but to my fearful and anxious heart I continually repeat: "Perhaps, perhaps, perhaps, the Lord will listen to the desires of the poor and his ears will hear the preparation of their heart!"[377] With special reference to one who is four days dead I will say: "Is your steadfast love declared in the grave or your faithfulness in perdition?"[378] If he will, our Savior may, without warning and in an unhoped for way, meet us and, moved by the tears if not the prayers of the mourners, he may restore the dead man to the living[379] or recall him from the very sepulchre,[380] I count a man dead when, defending his sins, he slips down to the eighth step. "From the dead, as from one who does not exist, confession ceases."[381] When he has passed the tenth step, the second after this, he is being carried away on the bier of reckless sin, he is expelled from the fellowship of the monastery. When he reaches the fourth of these last steps he is rightly said to be four days dead. Then a fifth step finds him hardened in sin, the grave closed over him.

56. God forbid that we should ever cease to pray for such men in our hearts even if we do not offer public prayers for them. St Paul prayed even for those whom he knew died impenitent.[382] For although they exclude themselves from the prayers of the faithful,[383] they can by no means exclude themselves from our affections. If only they would be warned of their terrible danger when they realize that the Church does not pray for them in her liturgy when she prays confidently even for Jews, heretics and pagans. For on Good Friday when

376. Ps 9bis:17.
377. Ps 87:11.
378. Ps 87:12.
379. Reference to the young man from Naim. See above, note 371.
380. An allusion to Lazarus.
381. Sir 17:26.
382. 2 Cor 12:21.
383. The "common prayer" or the prayers of the faithful are offered at the Eucharistic liturgy after the proclamation of the Gospel, the homily and the confession of faith, at the beginning of the part called the "mass of the faithful."

she prays for each class of sinners by name, she makes no mention of the excommunicated.[384]

A CONCLUDING NOTE TO THE RECIPIENT

57. Well, Brother Godfrey, you will, perhaps complain that I have not given you exactly what you asked and what I promised. It looks as if I had described the steps of pride rather than those of humility.[385] All I can say is that I can teach only what I know myself. I could not very well describe the way up because I am more used to falling down than to climbing. St Benedict describes the steps of humility to you because he had them in his heart; I can only tell you what I know myself, the downward path. However, if you study this carefully you will find the way up. If you are going to Rome who can tell you the way better than one you meet coming from there? He will describe the towns, villages, cities, rivers and mountains he has passed and as you go along you will meet and recognize them in the reverse order. So, we have described the stages of the downward road and you will see them as you climb up and down them better from your own experience than from the description of our book.

384. On Good Friday, when the central part of the mass, the re-presentation of Christ's saving death in the consecration of the bread and wine through the narration of the Lord's words from the Last Supper, is omitted, the other parts are more fully developed, especially the prayers of the faithful.

385. See above, Retractation, p. 25.

ON LOVING GOD

INTRODUCTION

ST BERNARD'S TRACT, *On Loving God,* is one of his
most delightful works. Beneath the rapid pace of the Latin rhythm, one can feel the powerful style of a great or-
ator, the deep thought of a serious mind and the mystical pene-
tration of a great saint. These qualities, however, fade in
brilliance before the abundant biblical quotations which seem
to flow like the current of a mighty river.

Historians have so far failed to come up with a precise date
for this work. All seem content to indicate the period between 1125, the year St Bernard is supposed to have written
his letter to the Carthusians,[1] and 1141, the year of Cardinal
Haimeric's death,[2] to whom the tract is addressed. It is interesting to note that the question which occasioned this
work came from the Pope's Chancellor, a leading personage
in politics at a time when the papal throne was the object
of considerable ambition and intrigue.

This tract is not a piece of scholastic theology. It is rather
a fine example of that spirituality which had developed in
the Church since the time of the Fathers. Its famous affirmation that God is to be loved without any limit, *sine modo,*

---

1. PL 182:109-115; Bruno Scott James, *The Letters of St Bernard of Clairvaux*
(Chicago: Henry Regnery Company, 1953), pp. 41-48.

2. Haimeric, Cardinal-Deacon, was born at Castres, near Bourges, France. He
was created Cardinal by Pope Callixtus II in 1121 and was appointed Chancellor
by Pope Honorius II in 1126, which post he held until death in 1141. St Bernard
addressed to him at least 14 letters as well as this tract. Clairvaux benefited by
his influence.

is borrowed from the letters of St Augustine.[3] Most of St
Bernard's doctrine comes from the Fathers and Holy Scripture.

To explain man's love for God, St Bernard gives as the
main reason St John's beautiful aphorism, "Because he loved
us first."[4] All that is good in man is seen as an expression of
God's love for him, with the obligation for man to love God
in return. Then follow man's motives for loving God: he cannot love any one more righteously or beneficially; God reconciled man to him by the death of his only Son; all man's
qualities are gifts from God. When man fails to appreciate
these gifts, he falls into ignorance, which makes him an animal,
or into arrogance, by which he resembles the demons who try
to usurp God's glory. A humble man attributes his qualities to
God who created man to his own image and likeness.

All men, even the infidels, should love God because all good
comes from him. Christians are obliged to love him for a still
greater reason: they need Jesus crucified. In a passage worthy
of the Fathers, St Bernard portrays the Church contemplating
her Redeemer's Passion, Death, and Resurrection, her heart
transfixed by the sword of love, as she utters the verse of the
Canticle: "Cushion me about with flowers, pile up fruit around
me, for I languish with love."[5] Fruit plucked from the tree of
life in her lover's garden symbolizes the sacrament of Christ's
Body and Blood which will produce immortal effects at the end
of time. The following verse: "His left hand is under my head
and his right hand will embrace me,"[6] is interpreted as meaning
the memory of God's graces received in this life helps man,
while God's right hand holds the fruits of the Resurrection
which are reserved for eternity.

Mankind is divided into two generations: the righteous
generation and the perverse one whose heart is unfaithful
to God. The righteous generation is portrayed by the
Bride reclining her head on the Bridegroom's left hand

3. The expression *sine modo* comes from a letter addressed to Saint Augustine
by his friend Severus, bishop of Milevis. See PL 33:419.
4. 1 Jn 4:9-10.
5. Song 2:5.
6. Song 2:6.

and remembering all the good she has received. This enables her to support the weight of the flesh which tends to drag her down to earth. Strengthened by these thoughts, she runs in the ardor of her love, yet she feels that even her deepest love is all too little because she is loved so much, for she is loved by God who loved man enough to give his only Son to save him. As man thinks of the joys God has prepared for those who love him,[7] that the sufferings of this life are nothing in comparison with the glory to come,[8] he asks what he can give God in return for such gifts.[9] God has an absolute right to all that man has and the fact of creation increases this debt, which is greater for Christians because they have been re-created by salvation, for grace restores the integrity which man lost through sin.

St Bernard now considers man in the light of charity which moves man to love God with all his heart, though he can never love God as much as he should. In this way he loves God as a reward but not on account of it. Charity cannot be bought or sold. This is the virtue which makes man free. The pursuit of wealth can never satisfy man's desires and only makes him more greedy. Thus the wicked walk in vicious circles.[10] Only those who thirst for justice will be satisfied. God alone can satisfy man's desires because he is the cause of man's love. He gives himself as food to holy souls; he sold himself in ransom for captive souls; he makes himself lovable so that man may not seek him in vain. If he is so for those who seek him, what must he be for those who find him?

After considering man's motives for loving God, St Bernard analyzes this love which he divides into four degrees. The first degree is that in which man loves himself for natural reasons. Later he learns that he cannot subsist without his neighbor, he has to rely on divine help when facing life's hardships, and he needs God's pardon when he sins. Thus man loves God for the good he has received, which constitutes the second degree of love. Since only a heart of stone could fail to see how lovable such a benefactor is, man moves on to the

7. 1 Cor 2:9.   9. Ps 115:12.
8. Rom 8:18.   10. Ps 11:9.

third degree of love in which God is loved for his own goodness. The fourth degree of love is different from the preceding ones. It is so perfect that the soul cannot love anything but God, it cannot even love itself except for God's sake. St Bernard says that such a degree of love may be possible during this life but only for a very short space of time. He believes that, as a state of life, the fourth degree is reserved for life after the resurrection of the body when the soul no longer feels the need of its mortal companion. Between death and the resurrection, the souls of the just are plunged into the ocean of eternal light, yet they still feel the need of the body for complete happiness.

St Bernard looks on man's three states of existence, on earth, after death, and after the resurrection of the body. He applies to them the verse of the Canticle: "Eat, O my friends, and drink; be inebriated, most beloved."[11] Souls toiling on earth are offered food; those reposing in death are invited to drink; and those full of love are let drink their fill. On earth, the just soul walks by faith working through love; its work is its food; "My meat is to do my Father's will."[12] After death the soul drinks wine weakened with milk; that is, its love for God is mixed with the desire to be reunited to the body. It is only when the soul grows unlike itself and starts to resemble God that it is allowed to drink the wine of wisdom, according to the psalm: "My cup inebriates me, how goodly it is."[13]

If wisdom presides over this triple banquet, it is charity that serves food to those who labor and drink to those who repose and inebriates those who reign. Only souls full of charity are invited to the wedding of the Lamb, eating and drinking at this table in his kingdom[14] when he takes to himself his Church in glory, without wrinkle, blemish or any such defect.[15] Those who love him most will be inebriated by the surpassing delights of his dwelling,[16] as the river's current which refreshes the city of God,[17] as the Son of God serving the elect the way he promised,[18] for "the just will feast and rejoice in God's presence exulting in their joy."[19]

11. Song 5:1.
12. Jn 4:34.
13. Ps 22:5.
14. Mt 26:29; Mk 14:25.
15. Eph 5:27.
16. Ps 35:9.
17. Ps 45:5.
18. Lk 12:37.
19. Ps 67:4.

The last four chapters of this tract are taken from St Bernard's letter to the Carthusians.[20] They constitute an admirable tribute in praise of charity and help interpret some difficult expressions in the preceding chapters. True charity proceeds from a pure heart, a peaceful conscience, and unfeigned faith,[21] by which a man loves his neighbor's good as well as his own. This is not the selfish love of the slave and the hireling but that of the son who does not seek his own advantage. This is the love which converts souls because it moves them to act willingly and not through the slave's fear or the hireling's greed. Where there is selfishness, there is a corner with its dust and rust that stain the soul. Charity is spotless and removes whatever separates the soul from God who is love.[22]

Charity is the law by which God lives. Man can possess it only as a gift from God. But God's love is substantial like everything that is in him, whereas human love is a quality which may be acquired or lost. God's love is always active and when man's will conforms to God's will, this love produces something of itself in man. Hence man can only love in God, that is in loving God first. The slave and the hireling seek to impose their own will, only to find themselves in the grasp of the most cruel of tyrants, man's own desires. Under this backbreaking yoke they plead to be freed from this body of death[23] to breathe under charity's light load. This happiness, however, is reserved for the son.

The last chapter contains a brief summary of the four degrees of love. Since man is the product of carnal desire, his love begins with that which is carnal. The facts of life show him he cannot subsist by himself and that he needs God's help. Thus he learns to love God as the giver of what he needs, which is the second degree of love. Through time man turns to God as the object of meditation, reading and prayer, a spiritual exchange in which God reveals himself gradually to man who learns how good God is. In this way man attains the third degree of prayer and probably remains there until the resurrection of the body. St Bernard maintains that the just, between their death on earth and the day of general judgment, enjoy eternal light but that they feel the urge to be reunited

20. See note 1.
21. 1 Tim 1:5.
22. 1 Jn 4:8.
23. Rom 7:24.

to their bodies for complete happiness. Having well served the soul on earth, the body deserves it share of glory.

The final paragraphs offer an apocalyptic vision of charity's net being dragged across the sea of time, catching all kinds of souls, until it is hauled on to the shore of eternity where the good will be separated from the bad forever and taken into heaven. There "everlasting joy will be theirs."[24]

One can conclude that this tract *On Loving God* occupies an important place in St Bernard's spiritual writings. For further evidence, one need only examine Etienne Gilson's book, *The Mystical Theology of Saint Bernard,* with its many quotations and paraphrases of texts from this tract. Mr Gilson gives a most enlightening analysis of St Bernard's theory of a Cistercian monk's progress from natural to supernatural love and points out how the Mellifluous Doctor was wise enough to avoid specifying when and how this change is made. He insists on the role of humility in the elimination of selfishness and in the acquisition of spiritual love which unites the soul to God and to one's neighbor. By this love, the soul rises under the guidance of the Holy Spirit to the degree of perfection it is to enjoy for all eternity.

Robert Walton, OSB

St-Benoît-du-Lac
P.Q., Canada

EDITORS NOTE

The translation presented here is based on the critical edition published by Jean Leclercq and Henri Rochais (see Bibliography). We have retained the subtitles as they are found in that edition. These titles, nine in number, are found in most of the manuscripts and go back to a very early date. In the manuscripts they are usually inserted in the text as in this translation; by way of exception they are sometimes listed at the head of the treatise.

I would like to take this opportunity to express publicly our gratitude to our Benedictine confrere for his most gracious collaboration in preparing the translation of this treatise and writing the introduction.

M. Basil Pennington, OCSO

24. Is 61:7.

PROLOGUE

TO THE ILLUSTRIOUS LORD HAIMERIC, Cardinal-Deacon and Chancellor of the See of Rome, from Bernard, Abbot of Clairvaux, wishing that he may live for the Lord and die in him.

UP TO NOW IT HAS BEEN YOUR CUSTOM to ask me for prayers and not for answers to questions. Let me confess I am not very apt at either, although my profession implies prayer even if my conduct falls short of my obligations. To be candid, I feel I lack the qualities which are requisite for that task: diligence and genius. Still, I am glad you are asking for spiritual favors in return for worldly gifts; however, you might have asked this of someone richer than I. Because both the educated as well as the uneducated have the habit of making excuses of this kind, and as it is not easy to affirm whether the excuse is prompted truly by ignorance or by modesty, unless it is proved in accomplishing the task imposed, accept from my poverty what I have, lest silence make me pass for a philosopher. I do not promise to answer all your questions, but only that which you ask, about loving God; even then my answer will be what he deigns to bestow on me. This subject tastes sweeter to the mind, is treated with more certainty, and is listened to with greater profit. Keep the other questions for more brilliant intellects.

ON LOVING GOD

YOU WISH ME TO TELL YOU why and how God should be loved. My answer is that God himself is the reason why he is to be loved.[1] As for how he is to be loved, there is to be no limit to that love. Is this sufficient answer? Perhaps, but only for a wise man. As I am indebted, however, to the unwise also,[2] it is customary to add something for them after saying enough for the wise.[3] Therefore for the sake of those who are slow to grasp ideas I do not find it burdensome to treat of the same ideas more extensively if not more profoundly. Hence I insist that there are two reasons why God should be loved for his own sake: no one can be loved more righteously and no one can be loved with greater benefit. Indeed, when it is asked why God should be loved, there are two meanings possible to the question. For it can be questioned which is rather the question: whether for what merit of his or for what advantage to us is God to be loved. My answer to both questions is assuredly the same, for I can see no other reason for loving him than himself. So let us see first how he deserves our love.

1. Cf. William of St Thierry: "Love is due to God only, and for no other reason than God himself."—*The Nature and Dignity of Love,* 3; PL 184-382; tr. G. Webb and A. Walker (London: Mowbray, 1956), p. 14.
2. Rom 1:14.
3. Bernard employs here a dictum common among Classical authors: . . . *sat est dictum sapienti.* See Plautus, *Persa* 4:7 (19); Terence, *Phormio,* 3:3 (8).

HOW GOD IS TO BE LOVED FOR HIS OWN SAKE

God certainly deserves a lot from us since he gave himself[4] to us when we deserved it least. Besides, what could he have given us better than himself? Hence when seeking why God should be loved, if one asks what right he has to be loved, the answer is that the main reason for loving him is "He loved us first."[5] Surely he is worthy of being loved in return when one thinks of who loves, whom he loves, how much he loves. Is it not he whom every spirit acknowledges,[6] saying: "You are my God, for you do not need my possessions."[7] This divine love is sincere, for it is the love of one who does not seek his own advantage.[8] To whom is such love[9] shown? It is written: "While we were still his enemies, he reconciled us to himself."[10] Thus God loved freely, and even enemies. How much did he love? St John answers that: "God so loved the world that he gave his only-begotten Son."[11] St Paul adds: "He did not spare his only Son, but delivered him up for us."[12] The Son also said of himself: "No one has greater love than he who lays down his life for his friends."[13] Thus the righteous one deserved to be loved by the wicked, the highest and omnipotent by the weak. Now someone says: "This is true for man but it does not hold for the angels." That is true because it was not necessary for the angels, for he who came to man's help in time of need, kept the angels from such a need,[14] and he who did not leave man in such a state because he loved him, out of an equal love gave the angels the grace not to fall into that state.

---

4. Gal. 1:4.
5. 1 Jan 4:9-10.
6. 1 Jn 4:2.
7. Ps 15:2 (Psalms are cited according to the Vulgate enumeration.).
8. 1 Cor 13:5.
9. The Latin text has *puritas* but, as W. Williams indicates, it means *caritas*: unmixed love. *Select Treatises of S. Bernard of Clairvaux*: De Diligendo Deo *and* De Gradibus Humilitatis (Cambridge: University Press, 1926), p. 10, n. 12.
10. Rom 5:10.
11. Jn 3:16.
12. Rom 8:32.
13. Jn 15:13.
14. Cf. Gra 29; OB 3:187; CF 19.

II.   2. I think that they to whom this is clear see why God ought to be loved, that is, why he merits to be loved. If the infidels conceal these facts, God is always able to confound their ingratitude by his innumerable gifts which he manifestly places at man's disposal. For, who else gives food to all who eat, sight to all who see, and air to all who breathe? It would be foolish to want to enumerate; what I have just said cannot be counted. It suffices to point out the chief ones: bread, sun and air. I call them the chief gifts, not because they are better but because the body cannot live without them. Man's nobler gifts—dignity, knowledge, and virtue—are found in the higher part of his being, in his soul.[15] Man's dignity is his free will by which he is superior to the beasts and even dominates them.[16] His knowledge is that by which he acknowledges that this dignity is in him but that it is not of his own making. Virtue is that by which man seeks continuously and eagerly for his Maker and when he finds him, adheres to him with all his might.

3. Each of these three gifts has two aspects. Dignity is not only a natural privilege, it is also a power of domination, for the fear of man hangs over all the animals on earth.[17] Knowledge is also twofold, since we understand this dignity and other natural qualities are in us, yet we do not create them ourselves.[18] Finally, virtue is seen to be twofold, for by it we seek our Maker and once we find him, we adhere to him so closely we become inseparable from him.[19] As a result, dignity without knowledge is unprofitable, without virtue it can be an obstacle.[20] The following reasoning explains both these facts. What glory is there in having something you do not know you have? Then, to know what you have but to be ignorant

15. Bernard defines what he understands by the soul in Conv 11: ". . . the whole of the soul is nothing other than reason, memory and will."—OB 4:84; CF 43.

16. Cf. Gen 1:26.

17. Gen 9:2.

18. In SC 37:5 (OB 2:11-12; CF 7) Bernard offers a moral evaluation of knowledge.

19. In SC 85:4 (OB 2:310; CF 40) Bernard defines virtue: *Est quippe vigor animi cedere nescius pro tuenda ratione; aut, si magis probas, vigor animi immobiliter stantis cum ratione vel pro ratione; vel sic: vigor animi, quod in se est, omnia ad rationem cogens vel dirigens.*

20. Cf. Bernard, Ep 372; PL 182:577; LSB, Letter 417, p. 485.

of the fact that you do not have it of yourself, for glory here, but not before God.[21] The Apostle says to him who glorifies himself: "What have you that you have not received? And if you have received it, how can you boast of it as if you had not received it?"[22] He does not say simply: "How can you boast of it," but adds: "as if you had not received it," to show the guilt lies not in boasting of something but in treating it as if it was not a gift received. This is rightly called vainglory, for it lacks the solid base of truth. St Paul marks the difference between true and vain glory: "He who boasts, let him boast in the Lord,"[23] that is, in the truth, for the Lord is truth.[24]

4. There are two facts you should know: first, what you are; secondly, that you are not that by your own power, lest you fail to boast at all or do so in vain. Finally, if you do not know yourself, do as is written: "Go follow the flocks of your companions."[25] This is really what happens. When a man, promoted to a high dignity, does not appreciate the favor received, because of his ignorance he is rightly compared to the animals with whom he shares his present state of corruption and mortality.[26] It also happens when a man, not appreciating the gift of reason, starts mingling with the herds of dumb beasts to the extent that, ignoring his own interior glory,[27] he models his conduct on the object of his senses. Led on by curiosity,[28] he becomes like any other animal since he does not see he has received more than they. We should, therefore, fear that ignorance which gives us a too low opinion of ourselves. But we should fear no less, but rather more, that which makes us think ourselves better than we are. This is what happens when we deceive ourselves thinking some good is in us of ourselves. But indeed you should detest and avoid even

21. Rom 4:2.
22. 1 Cor 4:7.
23. 1 Cor 1:31; 2 Cor 10:17. Cf. Jer 9:23-24.
24. Jn 14:6.
25. Song 1:6-7. Cf. SC 32:10; OB 1:233; CF 7.
26. Ps 48:13.
27. Cf. Ps 44:14.
28. For Bernard curiosity is the first step of pride: Hum 28, OB 3:38; see above, p. 57. Cf. also, Div 14:2; OB 6-1:135; CF 46.

more than these two forms of ignorance that presumption[29] by which you, knowingly and on purpose, seek your glory in goods that are not your own and that you are certain are not in you by your own power. In this you are not ashamed to steal the glory of another. Indeed, the first kind of ignorance has no glory; the second kind has, but not in God's sight.[30] But the third evil, which is committed full knowingly, is a usurpation of divine rights. This arrogance[31] is worse and more dangerous than the second kind of ignorance, in which God is ignored, because it makes us despise him. If ignorance makes beasts of us, arrogance makes us like demons. It is pride, the greatest of sins, to use gifts as if they were one's by natural right and while receiving benefits to usurp the benefactor's glory.

5. For this reason, virtue is as necessary as dignity and knowledge, being the fruit of both. By virtue the Maker and Giver of all is sought and adhered to, and rightly glorified in all good things. On the other hand, the man who knows what is good yet does not do it will receive many strokes of the lash.[32] Why? Because, "He did not want to understand to do well;"[33] worse again, "While in bed he plotted evil."[34] He strives like a wicked servant to lay hold of and even to steal his good Lord's glory for qualities which the gift of knowledge tells him most certainly are not from himself. Hence it follows that dignity without knowledge is quite useless and that knowledge without virtue is damnable. But the virtuous man, for whom knowledge is not harmful or dignity unfruitful, lifts up his voice to God and frankly confesses: "Not to us, O Lord, not to us, but to your name give glory;"[35] meaning, "O Lord, we attribute no part of our dignity or knowledge to ourselves: we ascribe it all to your name whence all good comes."

29. Likewise, presumption finds a place in Bernard's steps of pride as the seventh: Hum 44; OB 3:50; see above, pp. 72. Cf. also QH 11:4; OB 4:451; CF 43.

30. Rom 4:2.

31. Arrogance is Bernard's sixth step of pride: Hum 43; OB 3:49-50; see above, p. 71.

32. Lk 12:47.

33. Ps 35:4.

34. Ps 35:5.

35. Ps 113:9 (Vulgate: 113:1bis).

6. But see now, in trying to show that they who do not know Christ are sufficiently informed by natural law,[36] seen in the perfection of man's mind and body, to be obliged to love God for his own sake, we have lost sight of our subject. To state briefly what has been said, we repeat: is there an infidel who does not know that he has received the necessities for bodily life, by which he exists, sees, and breathes, from him who gives food to all flesh,[37] who makes his sun rise on the good and the bad, and his rain fall on the just and the unjust?[38] Who, again, can be wicked enough to think the author of his human dignity, which shines in his soul, is any other than he who says in the book of Genesis: "Let us make man to our own image and likeness?"[39] Who can think that the giver of knowledge is somebody different from him who teaches man knowledge?[40] Or again, who believes he has received or hopes to receive the gift of virtue from any other source than the hand of the Lord of virtue? Hence God deserves to be loved for his own sake even by the infidel who, although he is ignorant of Christ yet knows himself. Everyone, therefore, even the infidel, is inexcusable if he fails to love the Lord his God with all his heart, all his soul, all his might.[41] For an innate justice, not unknown to reason, cries interiorly to him that he ought to love with his whole being the one to whom he owes all that he is. Yet it is difficult, impossible for a man, by his own power of free will, once he has received all things from God, to turn wholly to the will of God and not rather to his own will[42] and keep these gifts for himself as his own, as it is written: "All seek what is their own,"[43] and further: ". . . man's feelings and thoughts are inclined to evil."[44]

III. 7. The faithful, on the contrary, know how totally they need Jesus and him crucified.[45] While they admire and embrace in him that charity which surpasses all knowledge,[46] they

36. Cf Rom 1:19ff; 2:14-15.
37. Ps 135:25.
38. Mt 5:45.
39. Gen 1:26.
40. Ps 93:10.
41. Mk 12:30.

42. See Gra 23; OB 3:103; CF 19.
43. Phil 2:21.
44. Gen 8:21.
45. 1 Cor 2:2.
46. Eph 3:19. Cf. Csi 5:28; OB 3:491; CF 37.

are ashamed at failing to give what little they have in return
for so great a love and honor. Easily they love more who
realize they are loved more: "He loves less to whom less is
given."[47] Indeed, the Jew and Pagan are not spurred on by
such a wound of love as the Church experiences, who says:
"I am wounded by love,"[48] and again: "Cushion me about
with flowers, pile up apples around me, for I languish with
love."[49] The Church sees King Solomon with the diadem his
mother had placed on his head.[50] She sees the Father's only
Son carrying his cross,[51] the Lord of majesty,[52] slapped and
covered with spittle; she sees the Author of life[53] and glory
pierced by nails, wounded by a lance,[54] saturated with abuse,[55]
and finally laying down his precious life for his friends.[56] As
she beholds this, the sword of love transfixes all the more her
soul,[57] making her repeat: "Cushion me about with flowers,
pile up apples around me, for I languish with love."[58]

WHENCE THE POMEGRANATES

These fruits are certainly the pomegranates[59] the bride introduced into her Beloved's garden. Picked from the tree of
life,[60] they had changed their natural taste for that of the
heavenly bread, their color for that of Christ's blood. At last
she sees death dead[61] and the defeat of death's author.[62] She
beholds captivity led captive[63] from hell to earth and from

47. Lk 7:43, 47; cf. 12:48.
48. Song 2:5 (Old Latin); cf. Song 4:9.
49. Song 2:5.
50. Song 3:11. Cf. Div 50:1; OB 6-1:270-271; CF 46.
51. Jn 19:17.
52. 1 Cor 2:8 (Old Latin).
53. Acts 3:15.
54. Jn 19:34.
55. Lam 3:30.
56. Jer 12:7; Jn 15:13.
57. Cf. Lk 2:35.
58. Song 2:5.
59. Song 6:10.
60. Gen 2:9.
61. Hos 13:14; cf. 1 Cor 15:54.
62. Heb 2:14.
63. Eph 4:8.

earth to heaven so that in the name of Jesus every knee must
bend in heaven, on earth and in hell.[64] She beholds the earth
which produced thorns and thistles under the ancient curse[65]
blooming again by the grace of a new blessing. And in all
this she thinks of the psalm which says: "And my flesh flour-
ished again; with all my will I shall praise him."[66] She wishes
to add to the fruits of the Passion which she had picked from
the tree of the Cross some of the fruits of the Resurrection
whose fragrance will induce the Bridegroom to visit her more
often.

  8. Then she says: "You are fair my Beloved, and handsome;
our couch is strewn with flowers."[67] By the couch she reveals
clearly enough what she desires and by declaring that it is
strewn with flowers, she indicates clearly whence she hopes
to obtain what she wants; not by her own merits,[68] but with
flowers picked in the field the Lord has blessed.[69] Christ loved
flowers; he willed to be conceived and raised in Nazareth.[70]
The heavenly Bridegroom enjoys so much those perfumes
that he enters willingly and often the chamber of the heart
he finds decked with these flowers and fruits. Where he sees
a mind occupied with the grace of his Passion and the glory
of his Resurrection, he is willingly and zealously present there.
Understand that the tokens of the Passion are like last year's
fruit, that is, of all the past ages spent under the domination
of sin and death,[71] until they appear in the fullness of time.[72]
But notice that the signs of the Resurrection are like this
year's flowers, blossoming in a new summer under the power
of grace. Their fruit will come forth in the end at the future
general resurrection and it will last forever.[73] As it is said:

64. Phil 2:10.
65. Gen 3:18; Heb 6:8.
66. Ps 27:7.
67. Song 1:15.
68. For Bernard's doctrine on merits, see SC 68:6; OB 2:200; CF 31.
69. Gen 27:27.
70. Bernard is alluding to the mystical or allegorical interpretation given to the
name, Nazareth. See Miss 1:3; OB 4:16; CF 43; Tpl 13: OB 3:225; CF 19.
71. Cf. Rom 5:21.
72. Gal 4:4.
73. In regard to the fruits of the Passion and Resurrection, see Ann 1:4; OB
5:15; CF 22.

"Winter is over, the rain is past and gone. Flowers appear in our land,"[74] showing summer has come back with him who changed death's coldness into the spring of a new life, saying: "Behold I make all things new."[75] His flesh was sown in death and rose again in the resurrection.[76] By his fragrance the dry grass turns green again in the fields of the valley; what was cold grows warm again and what was dead comes back to life.

9. By the freshness of these flowers and fruits and the beauty of the field giving off the sweetest of scents the Father himself is indeed delighted in the Son who is renewing all things, so that he might say: "Behold the odor of my son is as that of a rich field which the Lord has blessed."[77] Yes, a full field, of whose fullness we have all received.[78] But the spouse enjoys greater familiarity by the fact that when she feels inclined, she may gather flowers and fruit in this field and strew them over the depths of her conscience so that the couch of her heart will give off a sweet odor for the Spouse as he enters. If we wish to have Christ for a guest often, we must keep our hearts fortified by the testimony of our faith[79] in the mercy of him who died for us and in the power of him who rose from the dead, as David said: "These two things I have heard: power belongs to God and mercy to you, O Lord."[80] The testimonies of both these are ever so believable.[81] Christ died for our sins and rose again from the dead for our justification.[82] He ascended to heaven for our protection,[83] sent the Spirit for our consolation,[84] and will some day return for our fulfillment.[85] He certainly showed his mercy in dying, his power in rising again, and both of these in the rest.

10. These are the apples, these the flowers, with which the bride, feeling how easily the strength of her love can dwindle and weaken if it is not fortified by those stimulants, asks to be nourished and strengthened until she is introduced into

74. Song 2:11-12.
75. Rev 21:5.
76. 1 Cor 15:42.
77. Gen 27:27.
78. Jn 1:16.
79. Eph 3:17.
80. Ps 61:12-13.
81. Ps 92:5.
82. Rom 4:25.
83. Cf. Mk 16:19.
84. Cf. Jn 16:7; Acts 9:31.
85. Cf. Acts 1:11.

the Bridegroom's chamber.[86] There she will receive the long
desired caresses[87] and say: "His left hand is under my head
and his right hand has embraced me."[88] Then she will feel and
esteem all the signs of love she had received during her lover's
first visit,[89] as coming from his left hand, altogether inferior
and of little value in comparison with the infinite delights of
his right hand's embrace.[90] She will experience what she had
heard: "The flesh is of no use; it is the spirit that gives life,"[91]
realizing what she had read: "My spirit is sweeter than honey,
and my inheritance than honey and the comb."[92] What indeed
follows: "My remembrance will last for ages to come,"[93]
means as long as the present era lasts, in which a generation
arrives as the previous one passes away,[94] the elect will not be
deprived of memory's consolation until they can indulge in
the feast of God's presence. Thus it is written: "They will
publish the memory of your sweetness,"[95] no doubt meaning
those of whom it is said just before: "Generation after generation will praise your works."[96] Therefore, memory is for
the continuing ages, presence is for the kingdom of heaven,
where the elect are already glorified while remembrance consoles the present generation during its pilgrimage.

IV.   11. It is important to point out which generation finds
consolation in remembering God. Surely it is not the stubborn
and defiant generation[97] to whom it is said: "Woe to you who
are rich, you have your consolation,"[98] rather it is to the generation which is able to say: "My soul refused to be consoled."[99]

---

86. Song 2:5; 3:4. For Bernard's interpretation of the Bridegroom's chamber
see SC 23:3, 8-9; OB 1:140, 143-145; CF 7.
87. Prov 7:18.
88. Song 2:6. See below, no. 12, p. 40.
89. Cf. Adv 4:9; OB 4:182; CF 10.
90. Ps 30:20.
91. Jn 6:64.
92. Sir 24:27.
93. Sir 24:28.
94. Eccles 1:4.
95. Ps 144:7.
96. Ps 144:4.
97. Ps 77:8.
98. Lk 6:24.
99. Ps 76:3.

And we can accept the affirmation if one adds: "I was mindful of the Lord and delighted."[100] It is indeed right that they
who do not find pleasure in the joys of this life may think of
those to come and they who refused to be consoled by the
abundance of changing things, may delight in thoughts of
eternity. This is the generation of those who seek the Lord,
who do not seek for their own advantage[101] but for the face
of the God of Jacob.[102] In the meanwhile, memory is a pleasure for those who seek and long for God's presence, not that
they are completely satisfied but that they may long all the
more for him that they might be filled.[103] Thus he testifies
that he himself is food: "Who eats me, will hunger for more."[104]
Whoever is nourished by him says: "I shall be satisfied when
your glory appears."[105] Blessed are they who go hungry now
and thirst for justice, for they alone will be satisfied some
day.[106] Woe to you, false and corrupt generation! Woe to you,
foolish, stupid people,[107] who scorn his memory yet dread
his presence! Not even now do you want to be freed from the
hunter's net, since they who want to make money in this life,
fall into the devil's net.[108] Even then, you cannot avoid the
harsh words.[109] O the harsh and cruel sentence: "Depart accursed into everlasting fire."[110] Less harsh and less awful are
the words brought to our mind each day in the memorial of
the Passion: "He who eats my flesh and drinks my blood has
life everlasting."[111] That is, he who meditates on my death
and, following my example, mortifies his members which belong to this earth,[112] has eternal life;[113] meaning, if you share
in my sufferings, you will partake of my glory.[114] Many shrink

100. Ps 76:4.
101. 1 Cor 13:5.
102. Ps 23:6.
103. Cf. Mt 5:6. See Conv 26; OB 4:100-101; CF 43.
104. Sir 24:29.
105. Ps 16:15.
106. Mt 5:6.
107. Jer 4:22; 5:21.
108. Ps 90:3; 123:7; 1 Tim 6:9. Cf. Conv 14; OB 4:88-89; CF 43.
109. Cf. Jn 6:61.
110. Mt 25:41.
111. Jn 6:55. The reference is undoubtedly to the daily celebration of the Mass.
112. Col 3:5.
113. Jn 3:36.
114. Rom 8:17.

back at these words and abandon him,[115] saying by their re-
actions: "This expression is too hard, who can listen to it?"[116]
The generation which did not regulate its heart, whose spirit
is not in good faith with God[117] speaks this way and, setting
its hopes on futile riches,[118] feels oppressed by the message of
the Cross,[119] and judges the memory of the Passion a burden.
How will it ever bear the weight of these words in his presence:
"Depart accursed into the everlasting fire which was prepared
for the devil and his angels?"[120] This stone will crush him on
whom it falls.[121] However, the righteous generation[122] will be
blessed, for as with the Apostle, either present or absent,[123] it
seeks to please God. They will hear: "Come you blessed of
my Father, possess the kingdom prepared for you since the
beginning of the world."[124]

Then the generation which did not regulate its heart[125] will
learn too late how easy was Christ's yoke in comparison with
this sorrow and light was his burden[126] from which they with-
drew their stiff necks[127] as if it were a rough and heavy load. O
wretched slaves of Mammon,[128] you cannot glory in the Cross
of our Lord Jesus Christ[129] and at the same time trust in hoards
of money or chase after gold[130] and taste how sweet is the
Lord.[131] As a result, you will no doubt find him severe when
present, since you failed to remember him when absent.

12. On the other hand, the faithful soul sighs deeply for
his presence, rests peacefully when thinking of him, and must

115. Jn 6:67; 18:6.
116. Jn 6:61.
117. Ps 77:8.
118. 1 Tim 6:17.
119. 1 Cor 1:18.
120. Mt 25:41.
121. Mt 21:44.
122. Ps 111:2.
123. 2 Cor 5:9.
124. Mt 25:34
125. Ps 77:8.
126. Mt 11:30.
127. Deut 9:13; 31:27.
128. Mt 6:24.
129. Gal 6:14.
130. 1 Tim 6:17.
131. Ps 33:9.

glory in the degradation of the Cross[132] until it is capable
of contemplating the glory of God's revealed face.[133] Thus
Christ's bride and dove[134] pauses for a little and rests amidst
her inheritance after receiving by lot,[135] from the memory of
your abundant sweetness,[136] Lord Jesus, silver-tinted wings,[137]
the candor of innocence and purity, and she hopes to be filled
with gladness at the sight of your face,[138] where even her back
will glitter like gold[139] when she is introduced with joy into the
splendor of the saints.[140] There she will be enlightened by rays
of wisdom. Now she may glory and say: "His left hand is
under my head and his right hand embraces me."[141] His left
hand is symbolic of his unsurpassable charity which made him
lay down his life for his friends,[142] while his right hand portrays the beatific vision which he promised them and the joy
of his majestic presence. The vision of God which makes us
resemble him, and its incalculable delight are rightly figured
by the right hand, as the Psalmist joyfully sings: "In your
right hand are everlasting joys."[143] In the left hand is well
placed that admirable, memorable, and always to be remembered love, because the bride reclines on it and rests until
evil is past.[144]

13. In this way the Bridegroom's left hand is rightly under
the bride's head, so that, as she leans back, her head is supported on it, meaning the intention of her mind, lest bending
down it should be enticed by carnal and worldly desires.[145]
Because "the corruptible body weighs down the soul and
the earthly dwelling preoccupies the mind busy with many

132. Gal 6:14.
133. 2 Cor 3:18. Cf. OS 4:3; OB 5:357; CF 37.
134. Song 5:1-2.
135. Ps 67:14.
136. Ps 144:7.
137. Ps 67:14.
138. Ps 15:11.
139. Ps 67:14.
140. Ps 109:3.
141. Song 2:6.
142. Jn 15:13.
143. Ps 15:11.
144. Ps 56:2.
145. Gal 5:16; Tit 2:12.

thoughts."[146] What else is achieved by meditating on such great and so undeserved mercy, such gratuitous and so proved a love, such unexpected condescension, undaunted mildness, and astonishing kindness? What else, I insist, will all these carefully considered qualities achieve if they do not, in a wonderful way, captivate the mind of him who, completely freed from all unworthy love, considers them and attract it deeply so that it despises in comparison whatever cannot be desired without despising them? Then the bride surely runs more eagerly in the odor of their perfumes.[147] She loves ardently, yet even when she finds herself completely in love, she thinks she loves too little because she is loved so much. Nor is she wrong. What can requite so deep a love by so great a lover? It is as if a tiny grain of dust[148] were to gather all its strength to render an equal love to the Divine Majesty who anticipates its affection and is seen entirely bent on saving it. Finally, "God so loved the world that he gave his only begotten Son"[149] was no doubt spoken of the Father; and the words "He gave himself up"[150] were undoubtedly meant of the Son. It is said of the Holy Spirit: "But the Paraclete, the Holy Spirit, whom the Father will send in my name, will teach you all things and will make you remember all I have said to you."[151] God therefore loves, and loves with all his being, for it is the whole Trinity that loves, if the word *whole* can be said of the infinite, the incomprehensible, or indeed of a simple being.

V.   14. Whoever meditates on this is, I believe, sufficiently aware why man ought to love God, that is, whence God deserves to be loved. On the other hand, the infidel has neither the Father nor the Holy Spirit because he has not the Son.[152] "He who honors not the Son, honors not the Father who sent

146. Wis 9:15. This is a favorite quotation of Bernard, see Gra 37, 41 (OB 3:192-193, 196; CF 19); Conv 30 (OB 4:106; CF 43); Pre 59 (OB 3:292; CF 1:148); etc.
147. Song 1:3.
148. Is 40:15.
149. Jn 3:16.
150. Is 53:12.
151. Jn 14:26.
152. 1 Jn 5:12; cf. 2 Jn 9.

him,"[153] nor does he honor the Holy Spirit whom the Son sent.[154] Hence it is no wonder that he loves less him whom he knows less.[155] Nevertheless, even he is aware he owes him all whom he knows is the maker of all his being. What then should he be for me who hold my God to be not only the generous giver, the liberal administrator, the kindest consoler and the watchful governor of my life, but above and beyond that, the richest redeemer, the eternal defender who enriches and glorifies, as it is written: "With him is plentiful redemption;"[156] and also, "He entered the sanctuary once and for all, after winning eternal salvation."[157] The Psalmist says about our conversion: "He will not forsake his saints: they will be kept safe forever."[158] The Gospel says of enriching: ". . . good measure, pressed down, shaken up, and overflowing they will pour into your bosom;"[159] and again: "The eye has not seen, the ear has not heard, nor has the heart of man conceived what God has prepared for those who love him."[160] St Paul says of our glorification: "We are waiting for our Savior and Lord Jesus Christ, who will reform the body of our lowness, molding it into a likeness of his glorified body."[161] And again, "The sufferings of this life are not to be compared with the future glory to be revealed in us."[162] Better still: ". . . that which is but a passing, light tribulation in this life, produces in us a degree of glory beyond measure for the life to come, as we contemplate the things that are unseen, not those that are seen."[163]

15. What shall I render to the Lord for all these gifts? [164] Reason and natural justice urge the infidel to surrender his

153. Jn 5:23.
154. Jn 15:26; 16:7.
155. Cf. Lk 7:47.
156. Ps 129:7.
157. Heb 9:12.
158. Ps 36:28.
159. Lk 6:38.
160. 1 Cor 2:9.
161. Phil 3:20-21.
162. Rom 8:18.
163. 2 Cor 4:17-18.
164. Ps 115:12. Cf. Gra 48; OB 3:201; CF 19. This text was used at the Mass in reference to receiving the Eucharist.

whole being to him from whom he received it and to love him
with all his might. Faith certainly bids me love him all the
more whom I regard as that much greater than I, for he not
only gives me myself, he also gives me himself. The age of
faith had not yet come, God had not yet appeared in flesh,
died on the Cross, risen from the grave, or returned to the
Father. He had not yet commended his great charity in us[165]
about which I have said so much. Man had not yet been
ordered to love his Lord God with all his heart, all his soul,
and all his strength,[166] that is, with all he is, knows and can
do. Yet God is not unjust when he claims for himself his
works and gifts.[167] Why would not an artifact love its artist, if
it is able to do so? Why would it not love him all it can, since
it can do nothing except by his gift? In addition, the fact that
man was made out of nothing, gratuitously and in this dignity,
renders the debt of love clearer and proves the divine exaction
more just. Besides, how much did the benefit increase when
God, multiplying his mercy, saved men and beasts?[168] I am
speaking of us who exchanged our glory for the likeness of a
calf that eats grass,[169] who have become by sin like irrational
beasts.[170] If I owe all for having been created, what can I add
for being remade, and being remade in this way? It was less
easy to remake me than to make me. It is written not only
about me but of every created being; "He spoke and they were
made."[171] But he who made me by a single word, in remaking
me had to speak many words, work miracles, suffer hardships,
and not only hardships but even unjust treatment. "What
shall I render to the Lord for all that he has given me?"[172] In
his first work he gave me myself; in his second work he gave
me himself; when he gave me himself, he gave me back myself.
Given, and regiven, I owe myself twice over. What can I give
God in return for himself? Even if I could give him myself a
thousand times, what am I to God?[173]

165. Rom 5:8.
166. Deut 6:5; Mk 12:30 and parallel places.
167. Heb 6:10.
168. Ps 35:7-8.
169. Ps 105:20.
170. Ps 48:13, 21.
171. Ps 148:5.
172. Ps 115:12.
173. Cf. Job 9:3.

HOW GOD SHOULD BE LOVED

VI. 16. Briefly repeating what has been said so far, consider first how God merits to be loved, that there is to be no limit to that love, for he loved us first.[174] Such a one loved us so much and so freely, insignificant as we are and such as we are, that, as you recall I said in the beginning, we must love God without any limit. Finally, as love offered to God has for object the one who is immeasurable and infinite—for God is both infinite and immeasurable—what, I ask, should be the aim or degree of our love? What about the fact that our love is not given gratuitously but in payment of a debt? Thus the Immeasurable loves, the Eternal loves, that Charity which surpasses knowledge loves;[175] God, whose greatness knows no end,[176] to whose wisdom there is no limit,[177] whose peace exceeds all understanding, loves[178]—and we think we can requite him with some measure of love? "I shall love you, O Lord, my fortress, my strength, my refuge, my deliverer,"[179] and whatever can be held desirable and lovable for me. My God, my help, I shall love you as much as I am able for your gift. My love is less than is your due, yet not less than I am able, for even if I cannot love you as much as I should, still I cannot love you more than I can. I shall only be able to love you more when you give me more, although you can never find my love worthy of you. For, "Your eyes have seen my imperfections, and all shall be written down in your book,"[180] all who do what they can, even if they cannot do all they should. As far as I can see, it is clear enough to what extent God ought to be loved and that by his own merit. By his own merit, I say, but to whom is the degree of this merit really clear? Who can say? Who can understand it?

VII. 17. Let us see now how he is to be loved for our advantage. How far from the reality is our knowledge of it? Never-

174. 1 Jn 4:10.
175. Eph 3:19.
176. Ps 144:3.
177. Ps 146:5.
178. Phil 4:7.
179. Ps 17:2-3.
180. Ps 138:16.

theless, it is not right to keep silent about what has been seen, even if it falls short of the truth. When asking above why and how God is to be loved, I said the question may be understood in two ways: it may mean by what merit of his God deserves our love or what benefit do we acquire in loving him. Both questions it seems may be asked. After speaking of God's merit in a way no doubt unworthy of him, but according to the gift I have received, it remains for me, to speak of the reward in so far as it also will be given to me.

GOD IS NOT LOVED WITHOUT A REWARD

God is not loved without a reward, although he should be loved without regard for one. True charity cannot be worthless, still, as "it does not seek its own advantage,"[181] it cannot be termed mercenary.[182] Love pertains to the will, it is not a transaction; it cannot acquire or be acquired by a pact. Moving us freely, it makes us spontaneous. True love is content with itself; it has its reward, the object of its love. Whatever you seem to love because of something else, you do not really love; you really love the end pursued and not that by which it is pursued. Paul does not evangelize in order to eat; he eats in order to evangelize; he loves the Gospel and not the food.[183] True love merits its reward, it does not seek it. A reward is offered him who does not yet love; it is due him who loves; it is given to him who perseveres. When we have to persuade people in lesser affairs we cajole the unwilling with promises and rewards, not those who are willing. Who would dream of offering a man a reward for doing something he wants to do? No one, for example, pays a hungry man to eat, a thirsty man to drink, or a mother to feed the child of her womb.[184] Who would think of using prayers or prizes to remind a man to fence in his vine, to dig around his tree, or to build his own home? How much more the soul that loves God seeks

181. 1 Cor 13:5.

182. Bernard distinguishes mercenary love from that of the son, and also that of the slave. See below, no. 36, p. 127.

183. 1 Cor 9:18.

184. Is 49:15.

no other reward than that God whom it loves. Were the soul
to demand anything else, then it would certainly love that
other thing and not God.

18. Every rational being naturally desires always what satisfies more its mind and will. It is never satisfied with something which lacks the qualities it thinks it should have. A man
with a beautiful wife, for example, looks at a more attractive
woman with a wanton eye or heart; a well dressed man wants
more costly clothes; and a man of great wealth envies anyone richer than he. You can see men who already own many
farms and possessions, still busy, day after day, adding one
field to another,[185] driven by an excessive passion to extend
their holdings.[186] You can see men living in homes worthy of
a king and in sumptuous dwellings, none the less daily adding
house to house,[187] through restless curiosity building up, then
tearing down, changing squares into circles.[188] What about
men promoted to high honors? Do we not see them striving
more and more in an insatiable ambition to go higher still?
There is no end to all this, because no single one of these
riches can be held to be the highest or the best. Why wonder
if man cannot be content with what is lower or worse, since
he cannot find peace this side of what is highest or best? It
is stupidity and madness to want always that which can neither satisfy nor even diminish your desire. While enjoying
those riches, you strive for what is missing and are dissatis-
fied, longing for what you lack. Thus the restless mind, running to and fro among the pleasures of this life, is tired out
but never satisfied; like the starving man who thinks whatever he stuffs down his throat is not enough, for his eyes see
what remains to be eaten. Thus man craves continually for
what is missing with no less fear than he possesses with joy
what is in front of him. Who can have everything? A man
clings to the fruits of his work (however small they may be),
never knowing when he will have the sorrow of losing them,
yet he is certain to lose them some day.[189] In like manner a

185. Is 5:8.
186. Ex 34:24; Amos 1:13.
187. Is 5:8.
188. Horace, Ep 1:1 (100).
189. Cf. I Tim 6:7; Job 1:21.

perverted will contends for what is best, and hastens in a straight line toward what will afford it the most satisfaction. Rather vanity makes sport of it in those tortuous ways, and evil deceives itself.[190] If you wish to accomplish in this way what you desire, to gain hold of that which leaves nothing further to be desired, why bother about the rest? You are running on crooked roads and will die long before you reach the end you are seeking.

19. The wicked, therefore, walk round in circles,[191] naturally wanting whatever will satisfy their desires, yet foolishly rejecting that which would lead them to their true end, which is not in consumption but in consummation. Hence they exhaust themselves in vain instead of perfecting their lives by a blessed end. They take more pleasure in the appearance of things than in their Creator,[192] examining all and wanting to test them one by one before trying to reach the Lord of the universe. They might even succeed in doing so if they could ever gain hold of what they wish for; that is, if any one man could take possession of all things without him who is their Principle. By the very law of man's desire which makes him want what he lacks in place of what he has and grow weary of what he has in preference to what he lacks, once he has obtained and despised all in heaven and on earth,[193] he will hasten toward the only one who is missing, the God of all. There he will rest, for just as there is no rest this side of eternity, so there will be no restlessness to bother him on the other side. Then he will say for sure: "It is good for me to adhere to God."[194] He will even add to that: "What is there for me in heaven and what have I desired on earth, if you?"[195] And, also: "God of my heart, God, my lot forever."[196] Therefore, as I said, whoever desires the greatest good can succeed in reaching it, if he can first gain possession of all he desires short of that good itself.

20. This is altogether impossible because life is too short,

190. Ps 26:12.
191. Ps 11:9.
192. Rom 1:25.
193. Eph 1:10.

194. Ps 72:28.
195. Ps 72:25.
196. Ps 72:26.

strength too weak, competition too keen, men too fatigued by the long road and vain efforts; wishing to attain all they desire, yet unable to reach the end of all their wants. If they could only be content with reaching all in thought and not in deed. They could easily do so and it would not be in vain, for man's mind is more comprehensive and subtle than his senses. It even anticipates the senses in all things and they dare not contact an object unless the mind approves its utility beforehand. I think this is what is alluded to in the text: "Test all and hold on to what is good."[197] The mind looks ahead for the senses and these must not pursue their desires unless the mind gives its consent. Otherwise, you do not ascend the Lord's mountain or stand in his holy place,[198] because you have received your soul in vain, that is, your rational soul; while you follow your senses like a dumb beast, your sleepy reason offers no resistance. Those who do not think ahead run alongside the road,[199] they do not follow the Apostle's counsel: " . . . run, then to win . . . . "[200] When will they reach him whom they do not want to reach until they have tested all the rest? The desire to experience all things first is like a vicious circle, it goes on forever.

21. The just man is not like that. Hearing about the evil conduct of those who remain inside the circle[201] (for many follow the wide road which leads to death),[202] he prefers the royal road which turns neither to the right nor to the left.[203] Finally the Prophet confirms: "The path of the just is straight, and straight forward for walking."[204] These are the ones who take a salutary short-cut and avoid the dangerous, fruitless round-about way, choosing the shortened and shortening word,[205] not desiring everything they see, but rather selling all they have and giving it to the poor.[206] It is clear that "Blessed are the poor, for theirs is the kingdom of heaven."[207] All run, indeed,[208] but one must distinguish between runners. At length,

197. 1 Thess 5:21.
198. Ps 23:3-4.
199. Cf. Is 59:8.
200. 1 Cor 9:24.
201. Ps 30:14.
202. Mt 7:13.

203. Num 20:17;21:22.
204. Is 26:7.
205. Rom 9:28.
206. Mt 19:21 and parallels.
207. Mt 5:3.
208. 1 Cor 9:24.

"The Lord knows the way of the just, the way of the wicked will perish."[209] As a result, "Better is a little to the just than all the wealth of the wicked."[210] As Wisdom says and folly learns, money never satisfies those who love it.[211] Rather, ". . . they that hunger and thirst for justice will have their fill."[212] Justice is the vital, natural food of the rational soul; money can no more lessen the mind's hunger than air can that of the body. If you see a hungry man open wide his mouth to the wind and puff up his cheeks with air to satisfy his hunger, will you not think he is out of his mind? It is no less folly to think a rational soul will be satisfied rather than merely puffed up by any kind of material goods. What do material things mean to the mind? The body cannot live on ideas or the mind subsist on meat. "Bless the Lord, my soul, he satisfies your desires with good things."[213] He satisfies with good things, he incites to good, maintains in goodness, anticipates, sustains, fulfills. He makes you desire, he is what you desire.

22. I said above that God is the reason for loving God. That is right, for he is the efficient and final cause of our love. He offers the opportunity, creates the affection, and consummates the desire. He makes, or rather is made himself lovable. He hopes to be so happily loved that he will not be loved in vain. His love prepares and rewards ours.[214] Obligingly he leads the way; reasonably he requites us; he is our sweet hope. Rich for all who call on him,[215] although he can give us nothing better than himself. He gave himself to merit for us; he keeps himself to be our reward; he serves himself as food for holy souls;[216] he sold himself in ransom for captive souls.[217] O Lord, you are

209. Ps 1:6.
210. Ps 36:16.
211. Cf Eccles 5:9.
212. Mt 5:6.
213. Ps 102:1, 5.
214. Cf. 1 Jn 4:19.
215. Rom 10:12.
216. Wis 3:13.
217. For a fuller understanding of Bernard's doctrine on the Redemption by Christ, see Abael 14-15; PL 182:1064-1065. Vacandard sees in the previous phrase used here, "He gave himself to merit for us. . . ." (*se dedit in meritum*) the whole essence of Bernard's doctrine on the Redemption. See E. Vacandard, *Vie de saint Bernard, Abbé de Clairvaux*, 2 vols. (Paris:Lecoffre, 1895), 2:74. See also, W. Williams, "Introduction" in *Select Treatises*, pp. 4-5.

so good to the soul who seeks you,[218] what must you be to the one who finds you? More wonderful still, no one can seek you unless he has already found you. You wish to be found that you may be sought for, and sought for to be found. You may be sought and found, but nobody can forestall you. Even when we say: "In the morning my prayer will come before you,"[219] we must remember that, without our first receiving divine inspiration, all prayer becomes lukewarm. Let us now see where our love begins, for it has been shown where it ends.

VIII.   23. Love is one of the four natural passions.[220] There is no need to name them, for they are well known. It would be right, however, for that which is natural to be first of all at the author of nature's service. That is why the first and greatest commandment is: "You shall love the Lord, your God. . . ."[221]

THE FIRST DEGREE OF LOVE: MAN LOVES HIMSELF FOR HIS OWN SAKE

Since nature has become more fragile and weak, necessity obliges man to serve it first. This is carnal love by which a man loves himself above all for his own sake. He is only aware of himself; as St Paul says: "What was animal came first, then what was spiritual."[222] Love is not imposed by a precept; it is planted in nature. Who is there who hates his own flesh?[223] Yet should love, as it happens, grow immoderate, and, like a savage current, burst the banks of necessity, flooding the fields of delight, the overflow is immediately stopped by the commandment which says: "You shall love your neighbor as yourself."[224] It is just indeed that he who shares the same nature should not be deprived of the same benefits, especially that

218. Lam 3:25.
219. Ps 87:14.
220. Bernard frequently treats of the four basic passions; see, eg, SC 85:5; OB 2:310; CF 40; QH 14:9; OB 4:474; CF 43; Div 50:2; OB 6-1:271; CF 46; Quad 2:3; OB 4:361; CF 22. These are Classical; see, eg, Juvenal, *Satires* 1:85-86.
221. Mt 22:37.
222. 1 Cor 15:46.
223. Eph 5:29.
224. Mt 22:39.

benefit which is grafted in that nature. Should a man feel over-burdened at satisfying not only his brethren's just needs but also their pleasures, let him restrain his own if he does not want to be a transgressor. He can be as indulgent as he likes for himself providing he remembers his neighbor has the same rights. O man, the law of life and order[225] imposes on you the restraint of temperance, lest you follow after your wanton desires[226] and perish, lest you use nature's gifts to serve through wantonness the enemy of the soul. Would it not be more just and honorable to share them with your neighbor, your fellow man, than with your enemy? If, faithful to the Wiseman's counsel, you turn away from sensual delights[227] and content yourself with the Apostle's teaching on food and clothing,[228] you will soon be able to guard your love against "carnal desires which war against the soul"[229] and I think you will not find it a burden to share with those of your nature that which you have withheld from the enemy of your soul. Then your love will be sober and just if you do not refuse your brother that which he needs of what you have denied yourself in pleasure. Thus carnal love becomes social when it is extended to others.

24. What would you do if, while helping out your neighbor, you find yourself lacking what is necessary for your life? What else can you do than to pray with all confidence to him[230] "who gives abundantly and bears no grudges,[231] who opens his hand and fills with blessings every living being?"[232] There is no doubt that he will assist us willingly in time of need, since he helps us so often in time of plenty. It is written: "Seek first the kingdom of God and his justice, and the rest will be added thereto."[233] Without being asked he promises to give what is necessary to him who withholds from himself what he does not need and loves his neighbor. This is to seek the kingdom of God and implore his aid against the tyrany of sin, to prefer the yoke of chastity and sobriety rather than let sin reign in your mortal flesh.[234] And again, it is only right to

225. Sir 45:6.
226. Sir 18:30.
227. *Ibid.*
228. 1 Tim 6:8.
229. 1 Pet 2:11.

230. Acts 4:29; 28:31.
231. Jas 1:5.
232. Ps 144:16.
233. Mt 6:33; Lk 12:31.
234. Rom 6:12.

share nature's gifts with him who shares that nature with you.

25. Nevertheless, in order to love one's neighbor with perfect justice,[235] one must have regard to God. In other words, how can one love one's neighbor with purity, if one does not love him in God? But it is impossible to love in God unless one loves God. It is necessary, therefore, to love God first; then one can love one's neighbor in God.[236] Thus God makes himself lovable and creates whatever else is good. He does it this way. He who made nature protects it, for nature was created in a way that it must have its creator for protector. The world could not subsist without him to whom it owes its very existence. That no rational creature may ignore this fact concerning itself or dare lay claim through pride to benefits due the creator, by a deep and salutary counsel, the same creator wills that man be disciplined by tribulations so that when man fails and God comes to his help, man, saved by God, will render God the honor due him. It is written: "Call to me in the day of sorrow; I will deliver you, and you shall honor me."[237] In this way, man who is animal and carnal,[238] and knows how to love only himself, yet starts loving God for his own benefit, because he learns from frequent experience that he can do everything that is good for him in God[239] and that without God he can do nothing good.[240]

THE SECOND DEGREE OF LOVE: MAN LOVES GOD FOR HIS
OWN BENEFIT

IX. 26. Man, therefore, loves God, but for his own advantage and not yet for God's sake. Nevertheless, it is a matter of prudence to know what you can do by yourself and what you can do with God's help to keep from offending him who keeps you free from sin. If man's tribulations, however, grow in frequency and as a result he frequently turns to God and is frequently freed by God, must he not end, even though he had a heart of stone[241] in a breast of iron, by realizing that it is

235. Mk 12:30-31.
236. Mk 12:30.
237. Ps 49:15.
238. 1 Cor 2:14.

239. Phil 4:13.
240. Jn 15:5.
241. Ezek 11:19; 36:26.

God's grace which frees him and come to love God not for his own advantage but for the sake of God?

THE THIRD DEGREE OF LOVE: MAN LOVES GOD FOR GOD'S SAKE

Man's frequent needs oblige him to invoke God more often and approach him more frequently. This intimacy moves man to taste and discover how sweet the Lord is.[242] Tasting God's sweetness entices us more to pure love than does the urgency of our own needs. Hence the example of the Samaritans who said to the woman who had told them the Lord was present: "We believe now not on account of what you said; for we have heard him and we know he is truly the Savior of the world."[243] We walk in their footsteps when we say to our flesh, "Now we love God, not because of your needs; for we have tasted and know how sweet the Lord is."[244] The needs of the flesh are a kind of speech, proclaiming in transports of joy the good things experienced. A man who feels this way will not have trouble in fulfilling the commandment to love his neighbor.[245] He loves God truthfully and so loves what is God's. He loves purely and he does not find it hard to obey a pure commandment, purifying his heart, as it is written, in the obedience of love.[246] He loves with justice and freely embraces the just commandment. This love is pleasing because it is free. It is chaste because it does not consist of spoken words but of deed and truth.[247] It is just because it renders what is received. Whoever loves this way, loves the way he is loved, seeking in turn not what is his[248] but what belongs to Christ, the same way Christ sought not what was his, but what was ours, or rather, ourselves.[249] He so loves who says: "Confess to the Lord for he is good."[250] Who confesses to the Lord, not because he is good to him but because the Lord is good, truly loves God for God's sake and not for his own benefit. He does not love this way of whom it is said: "He will praise you when you do him favors."[251]

242. Ps 33:9.
243. Jn 4:42.
244. Ps 33:9.
245. Mk 12:31.
246. 1 Pet 1:22.

247. 1 Jn 3:18.
248. 1 Cor 13:5.
249. 2 Cor 12:14.
250. Ps 117:1.
251. Ps 48:19.

This is the third degree of love: in it God is already loved for his own sake.

THE FOURTH DEGREE OF LOVE: MAN LOVES HIMSELF FOR THE SAKE OF GOD

X. 27. Happy the man who has attained the fourth degree of love, he no longer even loves himself except for God. "O God, your justice is like the mountains of God."[252] This love is a mountain, God's towering peak. Truly indeed, it is the fat, fertile mountain.[253] "Who will climb the mountain of the Lord?"[254] "Who will give me the wings of a dove, that I may fly away to find rest?"[255] This place is made peaceful, a dwelling-place in Sion."[256] Alas for me, my exile has been lengthened."[257] When will flesh and blood,[258] this vessel of clay,[259] this earthly dwelling,[260] understand the fact? When will this sort of affection be felt that, inebriated with divine love, the mind may forget itself and become in its own eyes like a broken dish,[261] hastening towards God and clinging to him, becoming one with him in spirit,[262] saying: "My flesh and my heart have wasted away; O God of my heart, O God, my share for eternity."[263] I would say that man is blessed and holy to whom it is given to experience something of this sort, so rare in life, even if it be but once and for the space of a moment.[264] To lose yourself, as if you no longer existed, to cease completely to experience yourself, to reduce yourself to nothing is not a human sentiment but a divine experience.[265] If any mortal, suddenly rapt, as has been said, and for a moment is admitted to this, immediately the world of sin[266] envies him, the evil of the day disturbs him,[267] the mortal body weighs him down, the needs of the flesh bother him,

---

252. Ps 35:7.
253. Ps 67:16.
254. Ps 23:3.
255. Ps 54:7.
256. Ps 75:3.
257. Ps 119:5.
258. Mt 16:17.
259. 2 Cor 4:7.

260. Wis 9:15.
261. Ps 30:13.
262. 1 Cor 6:17.
263. Ps 72:26.
264. Cf. Gra 15; OB 3:177; CF 19.
265. Cf. Phil 2:7.
266. Gal 1:4.
267. Mt 6:34.

the weakness of corruption offers no support, and sometimes
with greater violence than these, brotherly love calls him back.
Alas, he has to come back to himself, to descend again into
his being, and wretchedly cry out: "Lord, I suffer violence,"[268]
adding: "Unhappy man that I am, who will free me from this
body doomed to death?"[269]

28. All the same, since Scripture says God made everything
for his own purpose,[270] the day must come when the work
will conform to and agree with its Maker. It is therefore necessary for our souls to reach a similar state in which, just as God
willed everything to exist for himself, so we wish that neither
ourselves nor other beings to have been nor to be except for
his will alone; not for our pleasure. The satisfaction of our
wants, chance happiness, delights us less than to see his will
done in us and for us, which we implore every day in prayer
saying: "...your will be done on earth as it is in heaven..."[271]
O pure and sacred love! O sweet and pleasant affection! O pure
and sinless intention of the will, all the more sinless and pure
since it frees us from the taint of selfish vanity, all the more
sweet and pleasant, for all that is found in it is divine. It is
deifying to go through such an experience. As a drop of water
seems to disappear completely in a big quantity of wine, even
assuming the wine's taste and color;[272] just as red, molten iron
becomes so much like fire it seems to lose its primary state;
just as the air on a sunny day seems transformed into sunshine
instead of being lit up; so it is necessary for the saints that all
human feelings melt in a mysterious way and flow into the will
of God. Otherwise, how will God be all in all[273] if something
human survives in man? No doubt, the substance remains
though under another form, another glory, another power.
When will this happen? Who will see it? Who will possess it?
"When shall I come and when shall I appear in God's pres-

268. Is 38:14.
269. Rom 7:24.
270. Prov 16:4; cf. Rev 4:11.
271. Mt 6:10.
272. Here again Bernard is taking his inspiration from the Mass where placing a
drop of water into the chalice of wine has an important signification.
273. 1 Cor 15:28.

ence?"[274] O my Lord, my God, "My heart said to you: my face has sought you; Lord, I will seek your face."[275] Do you think I shall see your holy temple?[276]

29. I do not think that can take place for sure until the word is fulfilled: "You will love the Lord your God with all your heart, all your soul, and all your strength,"[277] until the heart does not have to think of the body and the soul no longer has to give it life and feeling as in this life. Freed from this bother, its strength is established in the power of God. For it is impossible to assemble all these and turn them toward God's face as long as the care of this weak and wretched body keeps one busy to the point of distraction. Hence it is in a spiritual and immortal body, calm and pleasant, subject to the spirit in everything, that the soul hopes to attain the fourth degree of love, or rather to be possessed by it; for it is in God's hands to give it to whom he wishes, it is not obtained by human efforts. I mean he will easily reach the highest degree of love when he will no longer be held back by any desire of the flesh or upset by troubles as he hastens with the greatest speed and desire toward the joy of the Lord.[278] All the same, do we not think the holy martyrs received this grace, at least partially, while they were still in their victorious bodies? The strength of this love seized their souls so entirely that, despising the pain, they were able to expose their bodies to exterior torments. No doubt, the feeling of intense pain could only upset their calm; it could not overcome them.

XI. 30. But what about those souls which are already separated from their bodies? We believe they are completely engulfed in that immense ocean of eternal light and everlasting brightness.

THE CONDITION OF SOULS AFTER DEATH BEFORE THE RESURRECTION

But if, which is not denied, they wish that they had received their bodies back or certainly if they desire and hope to re-

274. Ps 41:3.
275. Ps 26:8.
276. Ps 26:4.

277. Mk 12:30.
278. Mt 25:21, 23.

ceive them, there is no doubt that they have not altogether
turned from themselves, for it is clear they still cling to something of their own to which their desires return though ever
so slightly. Consequently, until death is swallowed up in victory[279] and eternal light invades from all sides the limits of
night and takes possession to the extent that heavenly glory
shines in their bodies, souls cannot set themselves aside and
pass into God. They are still attached to their bodies, if not
by life and feeling, certainly by a natural affection, so that
they do not wish nor are they able to realize their consummation without them. This rapture of the soul which is its most
perfect and highest state, cannot, therefore, take place before
the resurrection of the bodies, lest the spirit, if it could reach
perfection without the body, would no longer desire to be
united to the flesh. For indeed, the body is not deposed or resumed without profit for the soul. To be brief. "The death of his
saints is precious in the sight of the Lord."[280] If death is precious, what must life be, especially that life? Do not be surprised if the glorified body seems to give the spirit something,
for it was a real help when man was sick and mortal. How true
that text is which says that all things turn to the good of those
who love God.[281] The sick, dead and resurrected body is a help
to the soul who loves God; the first for the fruits of penance,[282]
the second for repose, and the third for consummation. Truly
the soul does not want to be perfected, without that from
whose good services it feels it has benefited by in every way.

31. The flesh is clearly a good and faithful partner for a good
spirit, it helps if it is burdened; it relieves if it does not help;
it surely benefits and is by no means a burden. The first state
is that of fruitful labor; the second is restful but by no means
tiresome; the third is above all glorious. Listen to the bridegroom in the Canticle inviting us to this triple progress: "Eat,
friends, and drink; be inebriated, dearest ones."[283] He calls to

279. 1 Cor 15:54.
280. Ps 115:15.
281. Rom 8:28.
282. Mt 3:8.
283. Song 5:1. Cf. Gra 9; OB 3:172; CF 19; Div 41:12, 87:4; OB 6-1:253,331; CF
46.

those working in the body to eat; he invites those who have
set aside their bodies to drink; and he impels those who have
resumed their bodies to inebriate themselves, calling them his
dearest ones, as if they were filled with charity. There is a difference between those who are simply called friends, who sigh
under the weight of the flesh,[284] who are held to be dear for
their charity, and those who are free from the bonds of the
flesh, who are all the more dear because they are more ready
and free to love. More than the other two, these last ones are
called dearest and are so.[285] Receiving a second garment, they
are in their resumed and glorified bodies. They are that much
more freely and willingly borne toward God's love because
nothing at all remains to solicit them or hold them back. This
neither of the first two states can claim because, in the first
state the body is endured with distress, in the second state it
is hoped for as for something missing.

32. In the first state, therefore, the faithful soul eats its
bread, but, alas, in the sweat of its brow.[286] While in the flesh
it moves by faith[287] which necessarily acts through charity,[288]
for if it does not act, it dies.[289] Moreover, according to our
Savior, this work is food: "My food is to do the will of my
Father."[290] Afterwards, having cast off its flesh, the soul no
longer feeds on the bread of sorrow,[291] but, having eaten, it is
allowed to drink more deeply of the wine of love, not pure
wine, for it is written of the bride in the Song of Songs: "I
drank my wine mixed with milk."[292] The soul mixes the divine
love with the tenderness of that natural affection by which it
desires to have its body back, a glorified body. The soul, therefore, glows already with the warmth of charity's wine, but
not to the stage of intoxication, for the milk moderates its
strength. Intoxication disturbs the mind and makes it wholly
forgetful of itself, but the soul which still thinks of the resurrection of its own body has not forgotten itself completely.
For the rest, after finding the only thing needed, what is there

284. 2 Cor 5:4.
285. 1 Jn 3:1.
286. Gen 3:19.
287. 2 Cor 5:7.
288. Gal 5:6.

289. Jas 2:20.
290. Jn 4:34.
291. Ps 126:2.
292. Song 5:1.

to prevent the soul from taking leave of itself and passing into God entirely, ceasing all the more to be like itself as it becomes more and more like God? Then only, the soul is allowed to drink wisdom's pure wine, of which it is said: "How good is my cup, it inebriates me!"[293] Why wonder if the soul is inebriated by the riches of the Lord's dwelling,[294] when free from worldly cares it can drink pure, fresh wine with Christ in his Father's house?[295]

33. Wisdom presides over this triple banquet,[296] composed of charity which feeds those who labor, gives drink to those who are resting, and inebriates those who reign. As at an earthly banquet, edibles are served before liquid refreshments. Nature has set this order which Wisdom also observes. First, indeed, up to our death, while we are in mortal flesh we eat the work of our hands,[297] laboriously masticating what is to be swallowed. In the spiritual life after death, we drink with ease whatever is offered. Once our bodies come back to life we shall be filled with everlasting life, abounding in a wonderful fullness. This is what is meant by the Bridegroom in the Canticle saying: "Eat, my friends, and drink; dearest ones, be inebriated."[298] Eat before death, drink after death, be inebriated after the resurrection. It is right to call them dearest who are drunk with love; they are rightly inebriated who deserve to be admitted to the nuptials of the Lamb,[299] eating and drinking at his table in his kingdom[300] when he takes his Church to him in her glory without a blemish, wrinkle, or any defect of the sort.[301] By all means he will then intoxicate his dearest ones with the torrent of his delight,[302] for in the Bridegroom and bride's most passionate yet most chaste embrace, the force of the river's current gives joy to the city of God.[303] I think this is nothing other than the Son of God who in passing[304] waits on us as he in a way promised: "The just are feasting and rejoicing in the sight of God, delighting in their

293. Ps 22:5.
294. Ps 35:9.
295. Mt 26:29; Mk 14:25.
296. Prov 9:1ff.
297. Ps 127:2.
298. Song 5:1.

299. Rev 19:9.
300. Lk 22:30.
301. Eph 5:27.
302. Ps 35:9.
303. Ps 45:5.
304. Lk 12:37.

gladness."[305] Here is fullness without disgust; here is insatiable curiosity without restlessness; here is that eternal, inexplicable desire knowing no want. At last, here is that sober intoxication of truth, not from overdrinking,[306] not reeking with wine, but burning for God. From this then that fourth degree of love is possessed forever, when God alone is loved in the highest way, for now we do not love ourselves except for his sake, that he may be the reward of those who love him, the eternal recompense of those who love him forever.[307]

THE PROLOGUE FOR THE FOLLOWING LETTER

XII. 34. I remember writing a letter to the holy Carthusians some time ago and having discussed in it these same degrees of love along with other matters.[308] Perhaps I made some other remarks in it about charity but not different from what I say here. Hence I am adding the following passage to this tract as it appears useful, for it is easier to transcribe what has already been dictated than to compose something new.

HERE BEGINS THE LETTER ON CHARITY TO
THE HOLY BRETHREN OF CHARTRUSE[309]

I maintain that true and sincere charity proceeds from a pure heart, a good conscience and unfeigned faith.[310] It makes us care for our neighbor's good as much as for our own. For he who cares for his own good alone or more than for his neighbor's, shows that he does not love that good purely, that he loves it for his own advantage and not for the good itself. Such a man cannot obey the Prophet who says: "Praise the Lord, for he is good."[311] He praises the Lord indeed, because

305. Ps 67:4.
306. Cf. Acts 2:15.
307. See SC 83:4; OB 2:300; CF 40.
308. Ep 11; PL 182:108-115; LSB, Letter 12, pp. 41-48. See above, Introduction, pp. 85-90. From this point on, in the Latin text the word *caritas* is used in the place of *amor*.
309. The text here comprises Ep 11:3-9.
310. 1 Tim 1:5.
311. Ps 117:1.

he is good to him, but not because the Lord is good himself.
Let him be aware that the same Prophet addresses to him this
reproach: "He will acknowledge you when you do him a
favor."[312] A man can acknowledge that the Lord is powerful,
that the Lord is good to him, and that the Lord is simply good.
The first is the love of a slave who fears for himself; the second
is that of a hireling who thinks only of himself; the third is
that of a son who honors his father. He, therefore, who fears
and he who covets do so for themselves. Charity is found only
in the son. It does not seek its own advantage.[313] For this reason I think this virtue is meant in the text: "The law of the
Lord is spotless, it converts souls,"[314] for it alone can turn the
mind away from loving one's self and the world and fix it on
loving God. Neither fear nor love of self can change the soul.
At times they change one's appearance or deeds, they can
never alter one's character. Sometimes even a slave can do
God's work,[315] but it is not done freely; he is still base. The
hireling can do it also, but not freely; he is seen to be lured
on by his own cupidity. Where there is self-interest, there is
singularity;[316] where there is singularity, there is a corner;
where there is a corner, no doubt there is rust and dust.[317]
Let the slave have his own law,[318] the very fear which binds
him; let the hireling's be the lust for gain which restrains him
when he is attracted and enticed by temptation.[319] But neither
of these is without fault nor can either convert souls.[320] Charity converts souls because it makes them act willingly.

35. Then I have said charity is unspotted, it keeps nothing
of its own for itself. For him who holds nothing as his own,

312. Ps 48:19.
313. 1 Cor 13:5.
314. Ps 18:8.
315. Bernard employs here a term that has great meaning for the monk: *opus
Dei*, the work of God, the almost technical expression Benedict of Nursia employs
in his *Rule for Monasteries* to denote the monk's celebration of the praises of
God in choir through the day and night. See RB 43; 47; 58:7.
316. Singularity is Bernard's fifth degree of pride: Hum 42; OB 3:48-49; see above,
p. 70.
317. Cf VI p P 1:3; OB 5:208; CF 25.
318. Rom 2:14.
319. Jas 1:14.
320. Ps 18:8.

assuredly all he has belongs to God; and whatever belongs to God must be clean. Therefore, the unspotted law of the Lord is that love which does not seek what is useful to itself, but what is good for many.[321] It is called the law of the Lord either because he lives by it or because nobody possesses it except as a gift from him. It does not seem absurd for me to say God lives by a law, because it is nothing else than charity. What else maintains that supreme and unutterable unity in the highest and most blessed Trinity, if not charity? Hence it is a law, the law of the Lord, that charity which somehow holds and brings together the Trinity in the bond of peace.[322] All the same, let nobody think I hold charity to be a quality or a kind of accident in God. Otherwise, I would be saying, and be it far from me, that there is something in God which is not God. Charity is the divine substance. I am saying nothing new or unusual, just what St John says: "God is love."[323] Therefore, it is rightly said, charity is God, and the gift of God.[324] Thus charity gives charity; substantial charity produces the quality of charity. Where it signifies the giver, it takes the name of substance; where it means the gift, it is called a quality. Such is the eternal law which creates and governs the universe. All things were made according to this law in weight, measure, and number,[325] and nothing is left without a law. Even the law itself is not without a law, which nevertheless is nothing other than itself. Even if it does not create itself, it governs itself all the same.

XIII. 36. The slave and the mercenary have a law of their own[326] which is not from the Lord. The former does not love God and the latter loves something more than God. They have a law, I say, not the Lord's but their own, which is subject,

321. 1 Cor 10:33; 13:5.

322. Eph 4:3. Does Bernard have the Holy Spirit, the Third Person of the Blessed Trinity in mind here? It is not clear. In the next sentence he does affirm that he is not speaking of some accidental quality.

323. 1 Jn 4:8.

324. Eph 2:8.

325. Wis 11:21.

326. Rom 2:14.

all the same, to the Lord's law. Each one can make a law for himself, but he cannot withdraw it from the unchangeable order of the eternal law. I mean each one wants to make his own law when he prefers his own will to the common, eternal law. He seeks to imitate his Creator in a perverse way, so that as God is for himself his own law and depends on himself alone, so does man want to govern himself and make his own will his law. This heavy and unbearable yoke weighs on all Adam's sons,[327] alas, making our necks curve and bend down so that our life seems to draw near hell.[328] "Unhappy man that I am, who will free me from this body of death?"[329] by which I am weighed down and oppressed to the extent that, "Unless the Lord helped me, my soul would soon be living in hell!"[330] The soul struggling under this load laments saying: "Why have you set me against you, and I am become a burden for myself?"[331] By the words "I am become a burden for myself" is shown that he himself is his own law and that nobody but himself did that. But what he said previously, speaking to God: "Why have you set me against you" means that he has not escaped from God's law. It is proper to God's eternally just law that he who does not want to accept its sweet rule, will be the slave of his own will as a penance; he who casts away the pleasant yoke and light load of charity,[332] will have to bear unwillingly the unbearable burden of his own will. By a mysterious and just measure the eternal law has set its fugitive against himself yet retaining him captive, for he can neither escape the law of justice which he deserves nor remain with God in his light, rest, and glory, because he is subject to power and banished from happiness. O Lord, my God, "Why do you not take away my sin, and wherefore do you not remove my evil,"[333] that delivered from the heavy load of self-will, I may breathe under charity's light burden, that I may not be forced on by slavish fear or drawn on by a hireling's cupidity? May I be moved by your Spirit,[334] the

---

327. Sir 40:1; Acts 15:10.
328. Ps 87:4.
329. Rom 7:24.
330. Ps 93:17.

331. Job 7:20.
332. Mt 11:30.
333. Job 7:21.
334. Rom 8:14.

Spirit of liberty[335] by which your sons are acting, which bears witness to my spirit that I, too, am one of your sons,[336] that there is just one law for both of us, that I must also be as you are in this world.[337] For those who follow what the Apostle says: "May you owe nobody anything unless it be to love one another,"[338] without a doubt they are as God is in this world, neither slaves nor hirelings but sons.

XIV. 37. The sons are not without a law, unless a different meaning is given the text: "Laws are not made for those who are good."[339] It should be realized that a law of fear promulgated by a spirit of slavery[340] differs from that of gentleness given by a spirit of liberty. Sons are not obliged to obey a law of fear and they cannot exist without that of liberty. Do you wish to know why there is no law for those who are good? It is written: "But you have not received the spirit of servitude in fear."[341] Do you wish to hear that they are not without the law of charity? "But you have received the spirit of the adoption of sons."[342] Yet listen to the just man affirming of himself that he is not under the law, yet he is not lawless, "I have become," says he, "as if I was bound by the law with those who are bound by the law, although I am not bound by the law; and as if I was not bound by the law with those who are not bound by the law, although I am not without the law of God but bound by that of Christ."[343] It is not, therefore, right to say: "The just have no law," or "The just are without a law," but that "Laws are not made for those who are good,"[344] meaning they are not imposed on them unwillingly but, inspired by goodness, they are given freely to those who accept. Hence the Savior says so fittingly: "Take my yoke upon you,"[345] as if he said: "I do not impose it on the unwilling, but take it on you who desire it; otherwise, you will find toil instead of rest for your souls."

335. 2 Cor 3:17.
336. Rom 8:14, 16.
337. 1 Jn 4:17.
338. Rom 13:8.
339. 1 Tim 1:9.
340. Rom 8:15.
341. *Ibid.*
342. *Ibid.*
343. 1 Cor 9:20-21.
344. 1 Tim 1:9.
345. Mt 11:29.

38. The law of charity is good and sweet. It is not only borne gaily and easily, it also makes the laws of the slave and the hireling bearable, for it does not destroy them but fulfills them, as the Lord says: "I have not come to abolish the law but to fulfill it."[346] It tempers the slave's law and sets the hireling's in order, making both lighter. Charity will never be without fear but it will be a chaste fear; never without cupidity but it will be in order. Charity obeys the slave's law when it imparts devotion; it obeys the hireling's when it sets desires in order. Piety mixed with fear does not destroy fear; it chastens it. The punishment alone is taken away, without which fear could not exist while servile. But chaste and filial fear remains forever.[347] When one reads: "Perfect charity drives away fear,"[348] this must be understood of the punishment which is inseparable from servile fear; it is a figure of speech in which the cause is given for the effect. Cupidity in turn is set in right order by the arrival of charity, which moves one to reject evil altogether and prefer what is better to what is good, desiring what is good only on account of what is better. When this state is fully achieved, the body and all its good things are loved only on account of the soul, the soul on account of God, and God on account of himself.

XV. 39. Since we are carnal[349] and born of concupiscence of the flesh, our cupidity or love must begin with the flesh, and when this is set in order, our love advances by fixed degrees, led on by grace, until it is consummated in the spirit,[350] for "Not what is spiritual comes first, but what is animal, then what is spiritual."[351] It is necessary that we bear first the likeness of an earthly being, then that of a heavenly being.[352] Thus man first loves himself for himself because he is carnal and sensitive to nothing but himself. Then when he sees he cannot subsist by himself, he begins to seek for God by faith[353] and to love him as necessary to himself. So in the second degree of love, man loves God for man's sake and not for God's sake.

346. Mt 5:17.
347. Ps 18:10.
348. 1 Jn 4:18.
349. Rom 7:14.

350. Gal 3:3.
351. 1 Cor 15:46.
352. 1 Cor 15:49.
353. Heb 11:6.

When forced by his own needs he begins to honor God and
care for him by thinking of him, reading about him, praying
to him, and obeying him, God reveals himself gradually in
this kind of familiarity and consequently becomes lovable.
When man tastes how sweet God is,[354] he passes to the third
degree of love in which man loves God not now because of
himself but because of God. No doubt man remains a long
time in this degree, and I doubt if he ever attains the fourth
degree during this life, that is, if he ever loves only for God's
sake. Let those who have had the experience make a statement; to me, I confess, it seems impossible. No doubt, this
happens when the good and faithful servant is introduced
into his Lord's joy,[355] is inebriated by the richness of God's
dwelling.[356] In some wondrous way he forgets himself and
ceasing to belong to himself, he passes entirely into God and
adhering to him, he becomes one with him in spirit.[357] I believe the Prophet felt this when he said: "I shall enter the powers of the Lord; O Lord, I shall be mindful of your justice
alone."[358] He knew well that when he entered the spiritual
powers of the Lord, he would have to cast off all the infirmities of the flesh so that he would no longer have to think of
the flesh, but wholly in the spirit he would be mindful of
God's justice alone.

40. Then each member of Christ[359] can assuredly say of himself what Paul said of the Head: "If we have known Christ
according to the flesh, we no longer know him so."[360] Nobody
there knows himself according to the flesh because "Flesh and
blood will not possess the kingdom of God."[361] This does not
mean the substance of the flesh will not be present, but that
all carnal necessity will disappear, the love of the flesh will
be absorbed by that of the spirit and our present, weak, human affections will be changed into divine. Then charity's
net which is now being dragged across the broad and mighty
ocean of time, catching all kinds of fish, will be pulled ashore;

354. Ps 33:9.   358. Ps 70:16.
355. Mt 25:21.   359. 1 Cor 6:15.
356. Ps 35:9.   360. 2 Cor 5:16.
357. 1 Cor 6:17.   361. 1 Cor 15:50.

there the bad will be thrown away and only the good will be kept.[362] In this life, all kinds of fish are caught in charity's net, where, for the time being, it conforms to all,[363] drawing into itself the adversity and prosperity of all. In a way it makes them its own, rejoicing with those who rejoice, weeping with those who weep, as is its habit.[364] When the net reaches the shore, all that has been endured with displeasure will be thrown away like rotten fish, and only what could be a source of pleasure will be kept. For example, will Paul be sick with those who are sick, will he blush with those who are scandalized when sickness and scandal are taken away?[365] Will he weep for those who do not do penance where there is neither sinner nor penitent?[366] In that city whose river's current is a source of joy[367] and whose gates the Lord loves more than all the tents of Jacob,[368] let him never weep for those who have been condemned to eternal fire with the devil and his angels.[369] Even if at times victory causes rejoicing in other tents, one nevertheless must go into battle and often at the peril of one's life. However in that fatherland, no adversity or sorrow is allowed, for one sings of it: "All those who rejoice, dwell in you,"[370] and again: "Everlasting joy will be theirs."[371] Finally, how can mercy be remembered where one is mindful of God's justice alone?[372] Where there is no place for misery or time for mercy, there will surely be no feeling of compassion.

362. Mt 13:47-48.
363. 1 Cor 9:19.
364. Rom 12:15.
365. 2 Cor 11:29. Cf. 1 Cor 9:22.
366. 2 Cor 12:21.
367. Ps 45:5.

368. Ps 86:2.
369. Mt 25:41.
370. Ps 86:7.
371. Is 61:7.
372. Ps 70:16.

SELECT BIBLIOGRAPHY

SOURCES AND TRANSLATIONS

The Steps of Humility and Pride

Burch, G. Bosworth. *The Steps of Humility.* Text, trans., intro. and notes. Cambridge: Harvard University Press, 1940, 1942. Notre Dame: University Press, 1963.

Charpentier, R. *Traité de Saint Bernard des degrés de l'humilité et de l'orgueil* in *Oeuvres complètes*, vol. 2. Paris: Vives, 1866. Intro., pp. 412-413. Trans., pp. 414-456.

Leclercq, Jean and Rochais, Henri. *De gradibus humilitatis et superbiae* in *S. Bernardi opera* vol. 3. Rome: Editiones Cistercienses, 1963. Intro., pp. 3-11. Text, pp. 13-59.

Mabillon, Joannes. *De gradibus humilitatis et superbiae tractatus* in *S. Bernardi, Clarae-Vallensis abbatis primi, opera omnia*, vol. 1, PL 182. Paris, 1892. Intro., 939-940. Text, 941-972.

Mills, Barton R. V. *S. Bernardi tractatus de gradibus humilitatis et superbie* in *Select Treatises of S. Bernard of Clairvaux*, Cambridge Patristic Texts. Cambridge: University Press, 1926. Intro., pp. 70-74. Text with notes, pp. 75-156.

——*The Twelve Degrees of Humility and Pride.* Trans., intro. and notes. London: SPCK, 1929.

Ramos, G. Diez. *De los Grados de la Humildad y de la Soberbia* in *Obras Completas de San Bernardo*, vol. 2, Biblioteca de Autores Cristianos, 130. Madrid: Editorial Católica, 1955. Trans., pp. 882-930.

Solms. E. *Sur les degrés d'humilité et d'orgueil* in *Saint Bernard.* Namur: Soleil Levant, 1958. Intro. by J. Leclercq, pp. 12-15. Trans., pp. 16-86.

Webb, G. and Walker, A. *The Steps of Humility*, Fleur de Lys 13. Trans. and intro. London: Mowbrays, 1957.

On Loving God

Bégin, Albert. *Traité de l'amour de Dieu* in *Oeuvres mystiques.* Paris: Seuil, 1953. Pp. 27-82.

133

Charpentier, R. *Traité de l'amour de Dieu* in *Oeuvres complètes,* vol. 2. Paris: Vives, 1866. Intro., pp. 457-459. Trans., pp. 460-492.

Connolly, Terence L. *On the Love of God.* New York: Spiritual Book Associates, 1937. Techny, Illinois: Mission Press, 1943.

Gardner, Edmund Garrot. *The Book of St. Bernard on the Love of God.* New York: Dutton, 1916.

Lawson, Sr. Penelope. A Religious of CSMV. *On the Love of God.* London: Mowbrays, 1950.

Leclercq, Jean and Rochais, Henri. *Liber de diligendo Deo* in *S. Bernardi opera,* vol. 3. Rome: Editiones Cistercienses, 1963. Intro., pp. 111-117. Text, pp. 119-154

Mabillon, Joannes. *De diligendo Deo liber seu tractatus ad Haimericum S. R. E. Cardinalem et Cancellarium* in *S. Bernardi, Clarae-Vallensis abbatis primi, opera omnia,* vol. 1, PL 182. Paris, 1892. Intro., 971-974. Text, 973-1000.

Martin, H., ed. *On Loving God and Selections from Sermons.* London: SCM Press, 1959. Trans. by W. H. van Allen, pp. 15-64.

Patmore, Marianne Caroline and Coventry. *Saint Bernard on the Love of God.* London: Kegan Paul, 1881. London: Burns and Oates, 1884.

Ramos, G. Diez. *Del Amor de Dios* in *Obras Completas de San Bernardo,* vol. 2, Biblioteca de Autores Cristianos, 130. Madrid: Editorial Católica, 1955. Trans., pp. 742-776.

Solms, E. *Traité de l'amour de Dieu* in *Saint Bernard.* Namur: Soleil Levant, 1958. Intro. by Jean Leclercq, pp. 88-93. Trans., pp. 94-148.

Van Allen, W. H. *On Loving God,* Caldey Books, 1. Tenby: Caldey Abbey, 1909.

Williams, Watkin W. *S. Bernardi liber de diligendo Deo* in *Select Treatises of S. Bernard of Clairvaux,* Cambridge Patristic Texts. Cambridge: University Press, 1926. Intro., pp. 1-7. Text with notes, pp. 8-69.

STUDIES

Bouton, Jean de la Croix. *Bibliographie Bernardine 1891-1957,* Commission d'histoire de l'Ordre de Cîteaux 5. Paris: Lethielleux, 1958.

Bouyer, Louis. *The Cistercian Heritage.* Translated be E. Livingston. Westminster, Maryland: Newman. 1958.

Butler, Cuthbert. *Western Mysticism.* London: Constable, 1922. Reprinted New York: Harper & Row, 1966.

Delfgaauw, Pacifique. "La nature et les degrés de l'amour selon s. Bernard." In *Saint Bernard théologien. Analecta sacri ordinis cisterciensis* 9 (1953): 234-252.

Gilson, Etienne. *The Mystical Theology of Saint Bernard.* Translated by A. H. C. Downes. New York: Sheed and Ward, 1939.

Grill, Leopold, *"Epistola de charitate:* der älteste St.-Bernhards-Brief." In *Cîteaux* 15 (1964): 26-51; 386-388.

Hourlier, Jacques. "S. Bernard et Guillaume de Saint-Thierry dans le *'Liber de amore'.*" In *Saint Bernard théologien. Analecta sacri ordinis cisterciensis* 9 (1953): 223-233.

Janauschek, Leopoldus. *Bibliographia Bernardina. Xenia Bernardina,* vol. 4. Olms: Hildesheim, 1959.

Leclercq, Jean. "L'Art de la composition dans les traités de s. Bernard." In *Recueil d'études sur saint Bernard et ses écrits,* vol. 3. Rome: Storia e Letteratura, 1969. Pp. 105-162.

——"Pour l'histoire des traités de s. Bernard." In *Recueil d'études sur saint Bernard et ses écrits,* vol. 2. Rome: Storia e Letteratura, 1966. Pp. 101-130.

——"Pour l'iconographie de s. Bernard." In *Analecta sacri ordinis cisterciensis* 11 (1955): 145-146.

——"Le premier traité authentique de saint Bernard?" In *Recueil . . . ,* vol. 2. Pp. 51-68.

Luddy, Ailbe. *Life and Teaching of St. Bernard.* Dublin: Gill, 1927.

Mellet, P. *Notes sur le désire de Dieu chez saint Bernard.* Valais: N.-D. de Gérande, 1966.

Rousselot, P. *Pour l'histoire du problème de l'amour au moyen âge.* Baeumker Beiträge VI, 6. Münster, 1908. Paris, 1933.

Stoeckle, B. "Amor carnis—abusus amoris. Das Verständnis von der Konkupiszenz bei Bernhard von Clairvaux und Aelred von Rieval." In *Analecta Monastica* 7, *Studia Anselmiana* 54. Rome: Herder, 1965. Pp. 147-176.

Vacandard, E. *Vie de saint Bernard, Abbé de Clairvaux.* 2 vols. Paris: Lecoffre, 1895.

ABBREVIATIONS

Note: For references to Sacred Scripture the abbreviations found in the Revised Standard Version are employed. Abbreviated references for the Works of Bernard of Clairvaux are listed separately below.

CF Cistercian Fathers Series (Spencer, Massachusetts—Washington, D.C.: Cistercian Publications, 1970—)

EXP William of St Thierry, *Exposition on the Song of Songs*. CF 6 (1970)

LSB B. S. James, *The Letters of St Bernard of Clairvaux* (London: Burns & Oates, 1953)

OB *Sancti Bernardi opera*. Ed. Jean Leclercq, C. H. Talbot, H. M. Rochais (Rome: Editiones Cistercienses, 1957—)

PL *Patrologiae cursus completus, series Latina* (Paris, 1878—)

RB *Sancti Benedicti Regula Monasteriorum*. Ed. E. Manning (Westmalle, 1962). English version, L. J. Doyle, *St Benedict's Rule for Monasteries* (Collegeville, Minnesota: Liturgical Press, 1948).

ABBREVIATIONS FOR THE WORKS OF BERNARD OF CLAIRVAUX

Abael Ep de erroribus P. Abaelardi
Adv S. in adventu domini

Ann	S. in annuntiatione dominica
Asc	S. in ascensione domini
Conv	S. de conversione ad clericos
Csi	De consideratione libri V
Dil	L. de diligendo Deo
Div	S. de diversis
Ep	Epistola(e)
Gra	L. de gratia et de libero arbitrio
Hum	L. de gradibus humilitatis et superbiae
L	Liber
Miss	Homiliae super missus est in laudibus viriginis matris
Mor	Ep de moribus et officibus episcoporum
I Nov	S. in domonica I novembris
O Asspt	S. in dominica infra octavam assumptionis beatae Mariae viriginis
OS	S. in festivitate omnium sanctorum
Pent	S. in die sancto pentecostes
Pre	L. de precepto et dispensatione
QH	S. super psalmum Qui habitat
Quad	S. in quadragesima
S	Sermo (nes)
SC	S. super cantica canticorum
Tpl	L. ad milites templi (De laude novae militiae)
V Mal	Vita S. Malachiae

ANALYTIC INDEX

Numbers refer to paragraphs numbered in Arabic numerals in the text.
Hum = *The Steps of Humility; Dil* = *On Loving God.*

139

CISTERCIAN STUDIES SERIES

Under the direction of the same Board of Editors as the *Cistercian Fathers Series*, the *Cistercian Studies Series* seeks to make available to the English-speaking world significant studies produced in other languages, as well as various monastic texts and studies of perennial value with a view to placing the Cistercian Fathers in their full historical context and to bring out their present day relevance.

CISTERCIAN PUBLICATIONS
CONSORTIUM PRESS
Washington, D.C.
1974